Screen Goddesses

Hedy Lamarr in *Ziegfeld Girl* (1941). 'You stepped out of a Dream.'

Screen Goddesses

Daniel Cohen
Susan Cohen

Marilyn Monroe, even in the gaudiest of costumes, was able to project an air of sultry innocence.

**TIGER BOOKS INTERNATIONAL
LONDON**
A Bison Book

This edition published by
Tiger Books International Ltd.
London.

Produced by
Bison Books Ltd.
176 Old Brompton Road,
London, SW 5
England

ISBN 0 86124 168 1

Printed in Hong Kong

The fabulous Rita Hayworth was one of the most popular pin-up girls of World War II.

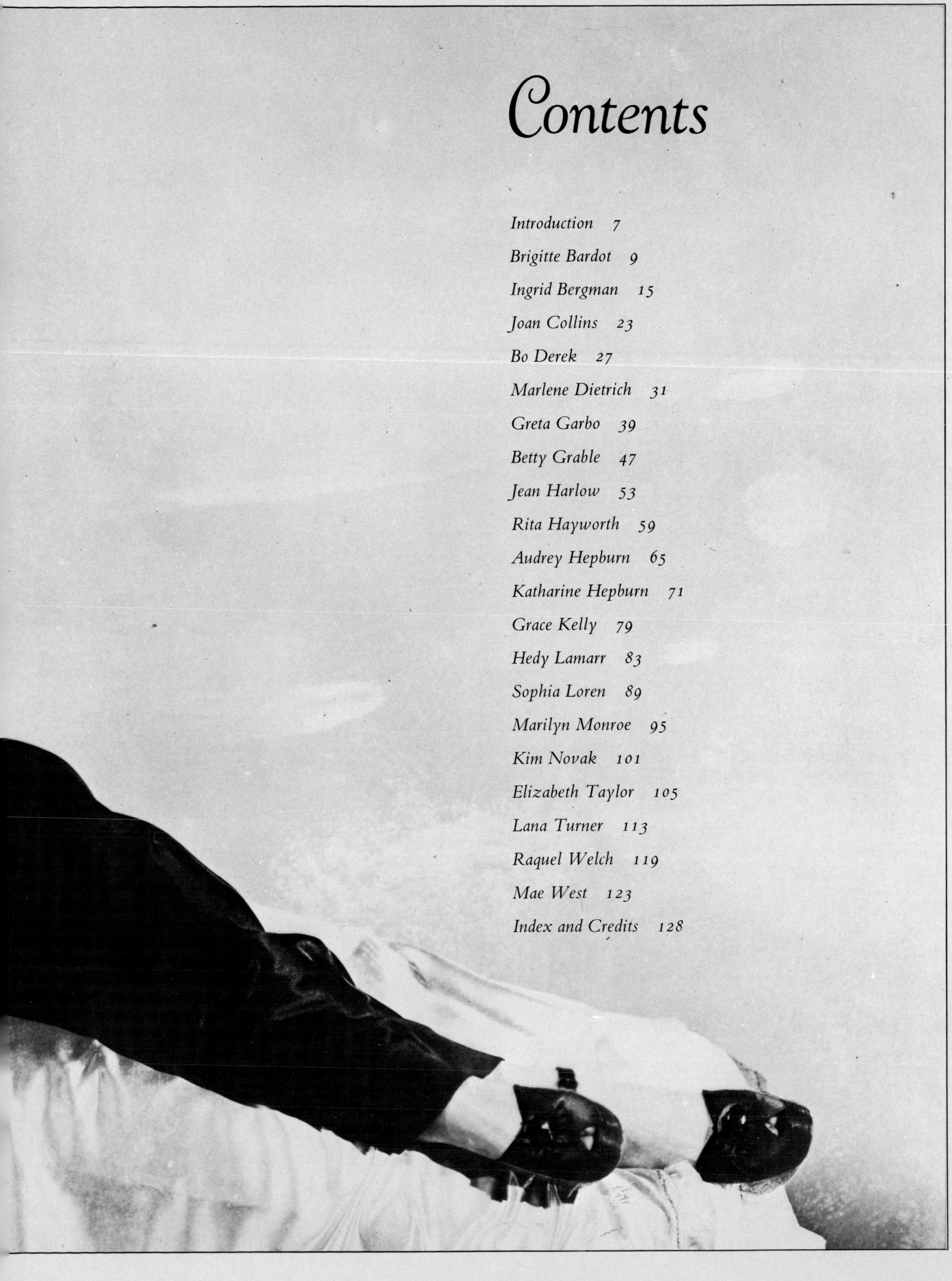

Contents

Introduction 7

Brigitte Bardot 9

Ingrid Bergman 15

Joan Collins 23

Bo Derek 27

Marlene Dietrich 31

Greta Garbo 39

Betty Grable 47

Jean Harlow 53

Rita Hayworth 59

Audrey Hepburn 65

Katharine Hepburn 71

Grace Kelly 79

Hedy Lamarr 83

Sophia Loren 89

Marilyn Monroe 95

Kim Novak 101

Elizabeth Taylor 105

Lana Turner 113

Raquel Welch 119

Mae West 123

Index and Credits 128

Introduction

*A*darkened movie theater and on the screen a shimmering silvery image or a technicolor vision. Screen goddesses: they are our dreams, our fantasies. We follow their careers, we read about their private lives. From brassy Mae West, whose 'come up and see me sometime' humor touched off an era of movie censorship in Hollywood, to cool and elegant Princess Grace Kelly, we love them.

The one thing they share is glamor but each in her own way is an individualist. Betty (Legs) Grable was so modest she cheerfully admitted that her acting abilities were nil. Elizabeth Taylor, a star since childhood, has lived her life in the full glare of publicity while Garbo was so secretive she wouldn't give MGM her phone number.

Sometimes our love turns to hate. Ingrid Bergman was a symbol of goodness and purity until her love affair with Italian film director Roberto Rossellini created a public furor. Denounced in the United States Senate, she was driven away from America for almost a decade.

Some of the symbols have faded. Kim Novak was one of the loveliest stars of the 1950s but most people under 30 do not know her name. Marilyn Monroe was legendary during the same era and she's mythic now. Lana Turner, 'the sweater girl,' and Rita Hayworth, 'the love goddess,' were products of the Hollywood studio system. Others, like the beautiful and mysterious Dietrich, arrived in Hollywood as legends in their own time. Sex kitten Brigitte Bardot, and the dazzling Sophia Loren, barely came to Hollywood at all. Some, like Raquel Welch, started as sex objects but survived as important talents. And some, like the elfin Audrey Hepburn, were symbols of romance.

In the darkness, our eyes on the screen, we submit. They charm us, angels and temptresses alike. The goddesses weave their magic spell.

Joan Collins was approaching the age of 50 before she became a genuine screen goddess.

Brigitte Bardot—the French 'sex kitten.'

Brigitte Bardot

She was the nymphette of the 50s, a playful and seductive sex kitten, who symbolized the self-indulgence and freedom from repression of the post-War world. Everyone has heard of her, even people who have never seen her films. In France she is a national treasure. It is a source of Gallic pride that the first non-Hollywood movie star to achieve world-wide recognition after World War II was Bardot (pronounced Bar-dough). They write about her, they gossip about her. There's even a name for this form of worship: Bardolatry. Bardot, with her mane of yellow hair, her lithe body, wonderful smile and adorable pout is a young man's dream and an old man's darling.

Brigitte Bardot was born in Paris in 1934. Her father was a rich industrialist and Bardot enjoyed the advantages which come with wealth. She took up modeling while studying ballet. In 1951 director Marc Allegret saw her picture on the cover of *Elle*, a popular French magazine, and he asked his assistant Roger Vadim to get in touch with her.

Vadim was enchanted with Bardot. He encouraged her to study acting. She took his advice, eventually appearing on stage, and she married Vadim in 1952. She had a few bit parts in films including a few English-language films as *Act of Love*, 1954, which starred Kirk Douglas. She was deliciously tempting in *Doctor at Sea*, 1955, with Dirk Bogarde. The part was minor but because the movie was so enormously popular millions had a glimpse of Bardot's special charm.

Stardom came quickly for Bardot. A series of mediocre films made her France's leading sex symbol within a year, and when Vadim was given the chance to direct and help write a vehicle for Bardot called *And God Created Woman*, 1956, her moment had come. *And God Created Woman* would make her an instant legend.

Bardot plays a juicy little sexpot but part of the movie's appeal is its setting: Saint-Tropez. These were the years when the Riviera was rediscovered and Bardot helped make it famous. She had a house in Saint-Tropez. In the public's mind she came to epitomize the new breed of rich young people living luxurious, glamorous and indolent lives in the South of France. Bardot, tanned, bikini-clad, treating sex as a natural taken-for-granted kind of thing, evoked a world of flashy sports cars, night life, and guilt-free promiscuity. She and Vadim were divorced and Bardot's name was often in the news because of her frequent love affairs.

Bardot's image and life style made her a hero to some, but she was a threat to others. Outside of France the respectable middle-class didn't approve of her. She seemed to set their values upside down. In this way, Bardot was ahead of her time. She had much in common with the generation that would follow hers, and which was responsible for the sexual revolution.

And God Created Woman made more than four million dollars in America and was one of the first foreign language films generally released in Britain after the War. In 1958 Bardot was the seventh biggest box office

draw in America. More movies followed with *En Cas de Malheur*, 1958, with Jean Gabin, her best. The scene used to advertise the movie showed Bardot raising her skirt to her stocking-tops. Bardot made *Babette Goes to War*, 1959, co-starring Jacques Charrier, whom she married. The couple had a son, but the marriage didn't last.

In 1960 France's famous intellectual, Simone de Beauvoir, wrote a treatise with the self-explanatory title, 'Brigitte Bardot and the Lolita Syndrome.' It was widely read and much-discussed. By now imitation Bardots seemed to people the planet. Though Bardot was not a teenager she was a trend-setter for them, and female adolescents aped her little girl womanliness.

However, despite the public view of Bardot as an eternal golden girl, her private world must have been very different, for on her 26th birthday she attempted suicide. She then made a movie called *Vie Privee*, 1962, which gave a biographical view of Bardot and her difficulties in dealing with her overwhelming success. Marcello Mastroianni co-starred.

In 1964 when Canada's *Weekend Magazine* estimated that her movies had brought 50 million dollars into France, Bardot at last made an American film. She played herself, appearing briefly in a James Stewart comedy called *Dear Brigitte*, 1964. Then she made *Viva Maria*, 1965, a Louis Malle comedy which also included Jeanne Moreau. Moreau and Bardot were superb together and the movie was an enormous hit in France. In 1966 Bardot married wealthy German Gunther Sachs but they were divorced.

Bardot's full-fledged English debut came in a British

Above: Even dressed in prim Victorian costumes, Bardot seemed to exude a sexiness mixed with innocence.
Below: Bardot used her body to make profitable films.

Bardot was discovered by director Roger Vadim, who considered her a pouty, well-endowed, playful ingenue.

Above: Bardot being discovered on the beach at St Tropez in *And God Created Woman* (1957).
Below: And God Created Woman was Bardot's debut in the US.

'Western' called *Shalako*, 1968, with Sean Connery. She played a French countess. She made more movies but there were fewer commercial successes.

Don Juan, 1973, directed by ex-husband Vadim, did not do well. She was still the 15th highest-paid French star and a sensation on television when she announced her retirement in the mid 1970s. The skeptics were wary but she meant the announcement. Attempts to lure her back failed. Her life, since retiring, however, has not been dull. She hasn't withdrawn from the world. Not long ago she went to Canada with a group of conservationists and animal lovers to try to prevent the clubbing to death of newborn seals, and she has supported other humanitarian causes.

Impishly sexy, a fun-loving gamin, the image of Brigitte Bardot as a female variant of Peter Pan endures. She is youth, she is joy, she is freedom.

Brigitte Bardot: *Act of Love* 54, *Doctor at Sea* 55, *The Light Across the Street* 55, *Helen of Troy* 55, *And God Created Woman* 56, *Heaven Fell That Night* 57, *Une Parisienne* 57, *En Cas de Malheur* 58, *Please Mr Balzac* 56, *The Devil is a Woman* 59, *Mam'selle Pigalle* 58, *Babette Goes to War* 59, *Please Not Now* 61, *The Truth* 61, *Vie Privee* 62, *Love on a Pillow* 62, *Contempt* 64, *Dear Brigitte* 64, *Viva Maria* 65, *Masculin Feminin* 67, *Two Weeks in September* 67, *Shalako* 68, *Novices* 70, *The Legend of Frenchy King* 72, *Don Juan* 73, *L' Histoire Tres Bonne et Tres de Colinet Trousse-Chemise* 73.

Above: Bardot starred with Marcello Mastroianni in *A Very Private Affair* (1962). It told the story of a successful movie idol (Bardot) and her thirst for privacy—obviously based on the life of Bardot herself.
Below: In *The Truth* (1960), Bardot was tried for murder and her defense attorney claims that it was a crime of passion. This was one of the few films in which she was permitted to show an unexpected acting range.

Ingrid Bergman and Gary Cooper starred in *For Whom the Bell Tolls* (1943). She was but 27 years old.

Ingrid Bergman

She had the most beautiful smile. She didn't need a ton of goo on her face or lacquered hair to look wonderful. Yet by the Hollywood standards of the 1930s she was all wrong and when David O Selznick first saw her he had grave doubts about her. She didn't care. Ingrid's intentions were always the same; to be an actress, not just a pretty face. Her one concession to Hollywood convention was to wear flat shoes so that at five foot nine she wouldn't look taller than her leading man. But she refused to wear make-up, or pose in a bathing suit for pictures. She was eager to play a wide range of good roles no matter how unglamorous, and preferred reading scripts and learning lines to partying and social climbing. Her list of screen credits reads like a *Who's Who* of best films and in the course of her career she received all kinds of awards, including three Oscars.

Ingrid Bergman, like Garbo, came from Sweden. She was born in Stockholm in 1915. Her mother was German, her father was Swedish. Most of her family were solidly middle-class and she absorbed many of their cherished values such as a passion for hard work, a sense of discipline, neatness and order. But, because her mother died when was was only two, the primary influence in her early life was her father, a talented artist and photographer with distinctly Bohemian views. He encouraged her to become an opera singer and though that was not to be, she knew from childhood on that she wanted to be an actress. She kept this ambition well into her teens even

after her father's death and no one could dissuade her. So at 18, despite family opposition, she auditioned for, and was accepted by, the Royal Dramatic Theatre School in Stockholm.

Ingrid did not stay at the school long, even though her talent was appreciated and she was chosen over more advanced students for a role on stage. The Theatre required a long apprenticeship and Ingrid had been offered a chance to work in films where leads came faster. She appeared in *Monkbrogreven/The Count of the Monk's Bridge*, 1934, a film comedy. Although one day the dress she wore in the movie's first scene would be displayed in the Museum of the Swedish Film Industry, there was no way to know at the time whether the decision to switch from theater to movies was wise. But, if there was one thing Ingrid understood, it was performing before a camera. She used to pose for her father in his photography shop when she was a child.

The Swedish movie industry was very low-key compared to Hollywood and Ingrid received excellent on-the-job training, appearing opposite some of the country's greatest actors in films with themes far more serious than Tinseltown would ever allow. In 1936 she made a romantic movie called *Intermezzo* which would ultimately prove her ticket to Hollywood. It was the story of a famous violinist who falls in love with a young pianist, played by Ingrid. Ingrid was now an important film star in Sweden and the American remake of *Inter-*

mezzo, 1939, with Leslie Howard as the violinist, would establish Ingrid as a star in the United States as well.

In 1937 Ingrid, now 21, married an attractive man of 30, Petter Lindstrom, a dentist who later became a doctor. He had known Ingrid before she was a star and had encouraged her in her career. Petter, like Ingrid, was hard-working and industrious. He was also a good skier, went jogging, knew how to box and was an excellent dancer. When Petter and Ingrid's daughter Pia was born he kept the child with him so Ingrid could go to Hollywood.

Ingrid had gone to Germany to make one movie, *Der Vier Gesellen*, 1938. It was supposed to be the first of four but she found Germany under the Nazis terrifying and refused to go back. Except for this one trip she knew little of life outside Sweden. But Ingrid could not have arrived in Hollywood at a better moment. Her naturalness, her radiant spiritual loveliness, was just what America wanted in a foreign star at that moment. By the 1940s she was the stand-in for all the good women of Europe, the virtuous victims of Hitler and the Nazis. It wasn't a part she played on screen but with her clean-cut charming young husband and her pretty little daughter she projected an image of wholesome femininity and fresh purity. Countless fans made her a symbol of hearth and home. This rosy picture of unreality was shattered later when Ingrid fell in love with Roberto Rossellini, the Italian film director, and the public turned against her in rage.

After *Intermezzo*, Ingrid went back to Sweden to rejoin her husband and child and make another movie there. She might never have worked exclusively in American films had it not been for the Second World War. The United States provided safety and of course there was no commuting to Europe in that bomb-ridden time. So Ingrid, Petter and Pia made America their home. In 1940 she was in New York, doing a play, *Liliom*. She had a long way to go to perfect her English and she knew her stage experience was inadequate, but she had supreme faith in herself and she never passed up an opportunity to enlarge her career.

She did a few movies on loan-out and when offered the part of the ingenue in *Dr. Jekyll and Mr. Hyde*, 1941, fought hard to get the part slotted for Lana Turner instead. She got her way and she and Lana literally swapped roles, with Ingrid playing the barmaid who becomes Hyde's most pathetic victim. The movie was excellent and she played very well against Spencer Tracy. Clearly, Ingrid knew how to choose a script. Nowhere was this gift more apparent than when she agreed to appear in a movie which had been turned down by several other actresses. The movie was *Casablanca*, 1942.

It was recognized as a masterpiece at the time and it's the film shown most frequently today on television. *Casablanca* just may be the most famous American movie ever made, even though no one would have expected

Above: Bergman starred in *Dr Jekyll and Mr Hyde* (1941). Here she is worrying about her relationship with Mr Hyde.

Below: In *Gaslight* (1944), Bergman starred with Charles Boyer in an exciting psychological melodrama about a man who is trying to drive his wife to insanity. For this role, she won her first Academy Award.

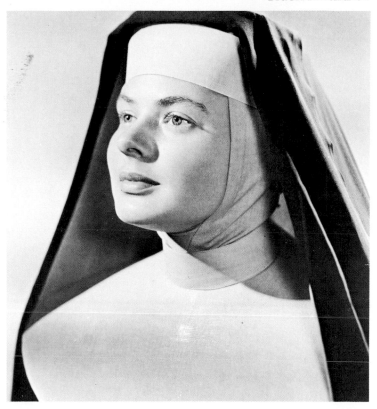

Above: Bergman as a nun in *The Bells of St Mary's* (1946).

Left: Bergman and Gregory Peck in Alfred Hitchcock's *Spellbound* (1945). She was his psychiatrist.

Below: Bergman about to make her famous getaway with Paul Henreid (rear) in *Casablanca* (1942). Humphrey Bogart and Claude Rains (in officer's uniform) helped.

Above: Bergman as *Anastasia* (1956), a part that won her her second Academy Award as best actress.

Below: Bergman and Yul Brynner in *Anastasia*, the story of a girl who thought she was the daughter of a Russian Czar.

such a thing during the filming. There was a lot of confusion on the set and the dialogue was written hastily. Nobody had the faintest idea how the movie would end until the last day of shooting. Humphrey Bogart played Rick, the cynical night club owner who comes to his true idealistic senses at the end, and Ingrid is the woman whose love he sacrifices to help the war effort. Ingrid felt the movie was moving and believable because the actors considered World War II their war. This wasn't just another picture to them.

Ingrid had wanted to play Maria, the Spanish peasant girl in *For Whom The Bell Tolls*, 1943, and Ernest Hemingway had agreed. But Paramount had hired a beautiful dancer named Vera Zorina, partly to save the cost of paying two star-sized salaries. Gary Cooper was the male lead. Money was always secondary to Ingrid. Even at the peak of her career she earned less than many other major stars but Selznick, who profited highly from loaning her out, did not share her attitude. So he set a stiff fee for her services.

When the film did not work out with Vera Zorina, Paramount asked for Ingrid Bergman. The film was an enormous success. Ironically, women all over America tried to wear their hair the way Ingrid did in the movie. It was a style which would have prevented a vain actress from accepting the part.

Gaslight, 1944, followed. Charles Boyer played a man deliberately trying to drive his wife insane. As the wife, Ingrid won her first Academy Award as 1944's Best Actress. Her next truly great film came in 1945. It was Alfred Hitchcock's *Spellbound*, an eerie suspenseful movie, one of Hitchcock's best. Ingrid played a psychiatrist. Gregory Peck is the amnesiac striving to unlock the vital secrets in his mind. *The Bells Of St Mary's*, 1945, meant Oscar number two. Bing Crosby was the priest, Ingrid the lively but dedicated nun. Women's clubs adored it and more than one devout mother looked upon the character Ingrid played as a role model for her daughters.

Ingrid was with Cary Grant in *Notorious*, Hitchcock again, 1946, another smash hit. She was now Hollywood's foremost female star, and she was to remain in the top ten for the following two years. David O Selznick would have been delighted to give her another contract but there were cracks in the facade of the studio system and Ingrid, who wanted more versatility, went free lance. She made the well-intentioned *Arch Of Triumph*, 1948, along with Charles Boyer and Charles Laughton, but the public refused to accept her playing a prostitute. They wanted Ingrid to be good.

Ingrid had never completely abandoned theater. She had played Eugene O'Neil's *Anna Christie* on stage in California, and had done Maxwell Anderson's *Joan of Lorraine* on Broadway. The character was based on Joan of Arc whom Ingrid had always found fascinating. She did a movie adaptation of the play, called *Joan Of Arc*,

1948, with Jose Ferrer, then appeared in *Under Capricorn*, 1949, an Alfred Hitchcock film set in Australia in the last century.

The war was over and Hollywood had rivals. Italy, decimated by the Second World War, was producing some of the greatest, most honest, and realistic films in the world. One of the finest of the new breed of directors was Roberto Rossellini whose *Open City* and *Paisan* made Ingrid Bergman realize how pale and static most Hollywood films were in comparison. She wanted desperately to work with Rossellini, believing that his genius and her talent would result in a film of high artistic achievement. She went to Italy to make *Stromboli*, 1950, with him. They fell in love. It was a passionate exciting affair and Ingrid became pregnant. The reaction to this in America is almost impossible to believe today.

It was the age of Joseph McCarthy and the Cold War was on in force. Anyone's loyalty could be questioned, their motives scrutinized. Along with the flag-waving patriotism went moralistic prudery. Ingrid Bergman, who had played both a nun and a saint, whose face shone with sincerity, honor and decency, was behaving like the bad girl in a bad movie as far as her fans were concerned. The public couldn't take it. Never mind that Ingrid, no more than any other actress, was not necessarily like the characters she played on film. Never mind that Ingrid and husband Petter lived very separate lives. Moviegoers felt betrayed. It was almost as if Ingrid's love affair with Rossellini was subversive.

Ingrid was to be punished for being human. *Stromboli* was banned in some places. Ingrid received hate mail. She and Rossellini were pursued by reporters and photographers. For a long time she was prevented from seeing Pia. On 14 March 1950, the Honorable Edwin C Johnson of Colorado delivered a scathing attack against Ingrid in, of all places, the United States Senate! This horrible nightmare didn't end with the birth of Ingrid's son, Roberto. Although Ingrid eventually received a divorce from Petter, married Rossellini and had two more children, twin girls, it was years before she was able to return to America. When she did she was fully vindicated and something of a heroine in the eyes of her embarrassed and sheepish fans.

Ingrid made more films with Rossellini but, artistically, the two talents were not a good mix. She was so very Nordic, he was so very Mediterranean. More successful was a theatrical production of *Joan Of Arc At The Stake*, an oratorio by Arthur Honegger, starring Ingrid, written by Paul Claudel, produced and directed by Rossellini. *Giovanna D'Arco* or *Joan at the Stake*, a 1954 film, based on the oratorio, also gained Ingrid attention. But life with the flamboyant and erratic Rossellini was taking its toll of Ingrid Bergman financially as well as emotionally. The marriage came to an end but there was a custody battle over the children.

20th Century Fox offered Ingrid a much needed two

Above: The very young, very beautiful Ingrid Bergman.

Below: Bergman in her last role—Golda Meir—in a made-for-television movie, *Golda*. She finished the film in pain and died soon afterwards of cancer.

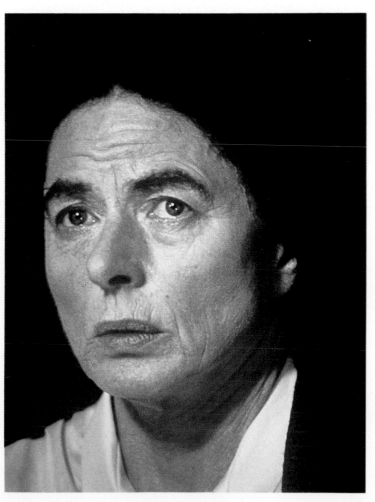

Above: Bergman as St Joan in *Joan of Arc* (1948).
Below: Bergman starred with Cary Grant in Alfred Hitchcock's *Nororious* (1946), which featured one of the most sensual kisses that had ever been seen on the screen up to that time. It was a top-notch World War II espionage tale set in South America.

hundred thousand dollars to play the title role in *Anastasia*, 1957, the story of a pretender to the throne of the Russian Czars. Ingrid made the movie in Britain and waited to see whether Americans would accept her. The movie was a popular success and she won an Academy Award for it as well as a New York Critics Award. The awards were America's way of saying, 'I'm sorry.'

In Europe she had done a lot of theater and Ingrid had improved as an actress. She continued to grow and develop as a talent, doing Ibsen, Shaw, Eugene O'Neill and Turgenev on stage. On screen she did *Indiscreet*, 1958, with Cary Grant, who had been a loyal friend during the whole Rossellini affair, and *The Inn of the Sixth Happiness*, 1958, the moving story of a dedicated missionary, who led a hundred Chinese children to safety during the Sino–Japanese War. Ingrid chalked up another success.

1958 was also the year she married Lars Schmidt, a Swedish producer and promoter who had worked in America and had offices in London, Paris and other European cities. The marriage was peaceful and lasted 12 years but the couple faced frequent separations because of their respective careers and so grew apart.

But Ingrid had her family. She was now close to daughter Pia once again and she was never at a loss for work. In 1964, she played the vindictive villain of *The Visit* and in 1969 she made *Cactus Flower* with Walter Matthau and Goldie Hawn. In 1972, while touring with George Bernard Shaw's *Captain Brassbound's Conversion*, she took the play to Washington DC and in the United States Senate, Senator Charles Percy of Illinois paid tribute to her graciousness and talent. Certainly, she deserved as much after the abuse she had received in the Senate 23 years earlier.

Ingrid was marvelous as the Swedish missionary in *Murder On The Orient Express*, 1974, which won her an Oscar for Best Supporting Actress. Perhaps her greatest screen triumph came in *Autumn Sonata*, 1978, with Liv Ullmann, when she played a world famous concert pianist who returns to Norway to see the two daughters she's neglected for years. The movie was directed by the great Swedish genius who shared the same last name, Ingmar Bergman. It is an extraordinary moving and disturbing film.

She did a play, *Waters of the Moon*, in London, 1979, at the historic Haymarket Theatre, and she was proud to perform there. Nothing could stop her, not even cancer. She continued working as long as she could. Her last great triumph came on television when she portrayed the Israeli prime minister, Golda Meir. When asked if she were nervous doing the role she answered that at first she was but then she saw an old friend, the camera, and everything was all right.

Yes, for Ingrid Bergman the camera was always her greatest friend.

Above: In *The Inn of the Sixth Happiness* (1958), Berman was a stoic missionary in pre-World War II China.
Below: Bergman's last film was *Autumn Sonata* (1978)—a collaboration of the two Swedish Bergmans—Ingrid and Ingmar.

Ingrid Bergman: *Monkbrogreven* 34, *Brannigar* 35, *Swedenhielms* 35, *Valborgsmassoafton* 36, *Pa Solsidan* 36, *Intermezzo* 36, *Juninatten* 40, *En Kvinnas Ansikte* 38, *En Enda Natt* 39, *Dollar* 38, *Die Vier Gesellen* 38, *Intermezzo* (US Remake) 39, *Rage in Heaven* 41, *Adam Had Four Sons* 41, *Dr Jekyll and Mr Hyde* 41, *Casablanca* 42, *For Whom the Bell Tolls* 43, *Gaslight* 44, *The Bells of St Mary's* 45, *Spellbound* 45, *Saratoga Trunk* 45, *Notorious* 46, *Arch of Triumph* 48, *Joan of Arc* 48, *Under Capricorn* 49, *Stromboli* 50, *Europa* 51, *We the Women* 53, *Journey to Italy* 54, *Joan at the Stake* 54, *Fear* 54, *Anastasia* 57, *Paris Does Strange Things* 57, *Indiscreet* 58, *The Inn of the Sixth Happiness* 58, *Goodbye Again* 61, *The Visit* 64, *The Yellow Rolls Royce* 65, *Fugitive in Vienna* 67, *Cactus Flower* 69, *A Walk in the Spring Rain* 70, *From the Mixed Up Files of Mrs Basil E Frankweiler* 74, *Murder on the Orient Express* 74, *A Matter of Time* 76, *Autumn Sonata* 78.

Joan Collins, the sultry British leading lady whose charms won her parts in international films and US TV.

Joan Collins

'A larger than life bitch.' That's how Joan Collins describes her role as Alexis in the hit TV series *Dynasty*. 'It's a great role,' she adds.

At, or nearing, 50, actress Joan Collins has achieved the sort of superstardom attained by very few, but it has come on television, not in films. Before she hit it big on *Dynasty*, Collins had a long film career. But a list of her credits, with few exceptions, reads like a list of forgettable films. Her Hollywood career had seemed just about over, but then for Joan Collins Hollywood had never been more than a second home.

She was born in London in 1933 (according to most official film histories). Her father was a theatrical agent and a partner with Lew (later Lord) Grade, one of England's most successful impresarios. Two of her aunts appeared regularly on the musical stage. So she had an early introduction to theater life and theater people. Early on Joan decided on an acting career and spent two years at the Royal Academy of Dramatic Art. She made her debut on the London stage in 1946 in Ibsen's *A Doll's House*. But she got more work as a model than as a stage actress. Her first major break came when she signed with the Rank organization. She made a string of films with names like *Cosh Boy* and *Turn the Key Softly*, both released in 1953. In these films Joan usually played the part of a sexy juvenile delinquent.

Joan's career may have been helped by her family's show business connections, but it was helped most by her own sultry beauty, which made her a standout even among the crowds of beauties who are attracted to film studios the world over. Yet there was also a hard edge to her looks which always seemed to land her 'bad girl' parts, from the early juvenile delinquents to *Dynasty*'s Alexis. She kidded herself by taking the part of the wicked witch in a TV production of *Hansel and Gretel*.

Joan's British films attracted attention in Hollywood— then the undisputed film capital of the world. She was signed by 20th Century Fox in the mid 1950s and immediately began appearing in major films. She had the title role in *The Girl in the Red Velvet Swing*, 1955, based on the celebrated case in which millionaire Harry K Thaw murdered architect Stanford White for having an affair with his showgirl wife, Evelyn Nesbitt. Collins was Nesbitt, a somewhat more sympathetic character than her usual role. It wasn't a part that called for a great actress. The main requirement was that she look gorgeous, which she most certainly did.

There were other big films like *Island in the Sun*, 1957 and *Rally Round the Flag Boys*, 1958 with Paul Newman. Oddly, the Joan Collins film that has had the most lasting appeal was a historical epic, *Land of the Pharaohs* 1955. Here she played the (guess what) evil Princess Nellifer, and winds up sealed inside of the Great Pyramid. This film, which was written by Nobel-prize winning author William Faulkner, has gathered a considerable cult following and is now regularly shown on TV and at film societies.

After her big start in the 1950s, Collins's career, while it certainly didn't end, did begin to wind down. She still worked regularly but the parts were smaller, the budgets

Above: The 22-year-old Collins with Richard Todd (as the ill-fated Sir Walter Raleigh) in *The Virgin Queen* (1955). Bette Davis played Queen Elizabeth I.

Below: Collins even made a TV appearance on *Batman*.

lower. Of course this was the 60s and all Hollywood was suffering from a television-induced slump. Joan Collins's last Hollywood credit was a flop called *Sunburn*, 1979. Still she kept busy, particularly in England, doing TV shows, some commercials and a few films. Some of these films like *The Stud* and *The Bitch*, were practically family affairs, for they were adapted for the screen from books by Joan's younger sister, Jackie, and produced by Joan's husband Ron Kass. As the titles indicate, they were not high class films.

Then in August 1981, when Joan was just at the point of returning to England permanently, she landed the *Dynasty* part, and her presence pushed the floundering series right to the top of the ratings.

Off screen Joan developed a reputation for being outspoken. Shortly after she arrived in Hollywood she said, 'In London they kept saying learn to be an actress. In Hollywood they say you're great when they mean you are good, and they say you're good when they mean you're awful.'

Recently in reflecting on her long film career she admitted, 'Okay, as a body of work over the years it is not that fantastic, but I did get some not too shabby reviews in some fairly mediocre films. I can cut the mustard as an actress in more ways than people have given me credit for.'

Sometimes her outspokenness has gotten her in trouble. In her autobiography *Past Imperfect* she detailed her affairs with everyone from actor Ryan O'Neal to Dominican Republic dictator Rafael Trujillo. The book created such a negative reaction in England that Joan returned a $100,000 advance so that the book would not appear in the US. Now, however, her *Dynasty* fame, and the vast profits that might be expected from such a book, has made her reconsider. 'Show me a person for whom money is no issue and I'll show you a billionaire,' she says.

In one way Joan Collins is unique among screen goddesses. Many can not survive no longer being young but Joan is probably a bigger sex symbol today than she was when she started in pictures over 30 years ago. Joan Collins doesn't just look good for a woman of 50, she looks great for a woman of any age.

Joan Collins: *I Believe in You* 52, *Cosh Boy* 53, *Our Girl Friday* 53, *Turn the Key Softly* 53, *The Good Die Young* 54, *Land of the Pharaohs* 55, *The Virgin Queen* 55, *The Girl in the Red Velvet Swing* 55, *The Opposite Sex* 56, *The Wayward Bus* 57, *Island in the Sun* 57, *Sea Wife* 57, *The Bravados* 58, *Rally Round the Flag Boys* 58, *Seven Thieves* 60, *Road to Hong Kong* 62, *Warning Shot* 66, *Heironymus Merkin* 69, *The Executioner* 69, *Up in the Cellar* 70, *Drive Hard, Drive Fast* 70, *Quest for Love* 71, *Revenge* 71, *Tales that Witness Madness* 73, *Alfie Darling* 74, *I Don't Want to be Born* 75, *Sunburn* 79.

As she approached 50, Joan Collins suddenly became a sex symbol and made a few soft-core porno movies.

Bo Derek—America's newest heart-throb and fantasy woman.

Bo Derek

In late 1979 and 1980 women all over America were wearing their hair in tiny beaded braids. This elaborate and difficult hairstyle was known as cornrows. The cornrow style had been around for centuries, and had always been popular among Africans. But it wasn't a surging interest in African fashion that brought on the US fad. It was that the cornrow hairstyle had been worn by a spectacular new 22-year-old sex symbol named Bo Derek.

Few actresses have ever attracted so much instant attention. Bo had appeared in only one film, a lightweight, but extremely popular comedy called '10'. She wasn't the star. The star was the diminuitive British comedian Dudley Moore. The film did a lot for Moore's career too, but he had been around for quite a while already. She wasn't the female lead. That was played by Julie Andrews, though practically no one remembers that she was in the film. Bo is the sexy, uninhibited 'other woman.' She is on screen for less than 15 minutes, much of that time wearing only her celebrated cornrow hairstyle. She was a phenomenon, 10 on a scale of 10, perhaps 11.

By 1979 when '10' was made, on-screen nudity was no novelty, as it had been back when Hedy Lamarr appeared nude in *Ecstasy*. It took more than that to attract attention.

Is there some sort of mysterious chemistry, or is it careful packaging that makes the public respond to one screen personality over a horde of others? It's probably a bit of both. Bo had the chemistry, but she had the packaging as well.

Her packager, mentor, guru and husband was John Derek. Derek had once been a pretty boy actor but after his own career ended he turned to producing films and to promoting the careers of beautiful women who he married. Ursula Andress was his second wife, Linda Evans his third.

Derek first met Bo when she was a 16-year-old high school dropout named Mary Cathleen Collins. He thought she would be perfect for a small part in a low budget film he was producing in Greece. (The film called *Love You* has never been released). The star of *Love You* was Mrs Derek III, Linda Evans. By the time the film was finished, Bo had replaced Linda in John's stable. They finally married in 1977.

After the Greek episode Bo didn't work in films until director Blake Edwards picked her for the part in '10' and this came as a surprise to both John and Bo. And everybody concerned was surprised at the fantastic impact she made in the film. It wasn't supposed to be a major role and she got only $35,000 for it.

For her next film, *A Change of Seasons*, 1980, she got $100,000. In this film which stars Shirley MacLaine and Anthony Hopkins, Bo again plays the other woman, a

Derek with her co-stars, Miles O'Keefe and an ape, in *Tarzan, The Ape Man* (1981).

student who has fallen for her professor. This time she appears nude in a hot tub. The picture was practically unnoticed.

What everyone was waiting for was Bo's next film, *Tarzan, The Ape Man*, for it was to be her splashiest vehicle. And it was to be completely a Derek production. *Tarzan*, 1981, was a remake of the 1932 classic with Maureen O'Sullivan and Johnny Weissmuller. The title role was given to an unknown muscular former boxer named Lee Canalito. But the focus of the picture had been shifted from Tarzan to Jane, and often Jane wore less than the ape man himself.

The Dereks responded to the rather sinister gossip about John controlling Bo's life by naming their production company Svengali Inc, with Bo, not John, taking the title of President. Company notepaper had a drawing of Bo manipulating a puppet of John.

Tarzan had a tremendous amount of pre-release publicity. When it came out, the critics, predictably, were gunning for it. Only the ape got good reviews.

Often the public responds very differently than the critics. But in regards to *Tarzan* there was a rare meeting of the minds. The picture was just too silly. Bo had plenty of opportunity to display her famous but now increasingly familiar body. It wasn't enough.

Will Bo Derek become the sex symbol of the '80s as many once predicted—or a footnote to film history. Says Blake Edwards, 'Bo may become a superstar if she escapes being thrown into roles that are wrong for her. But in this business all you need is a couple of bad pictures and your career is over as suddenly as it began.'

Bo Derek: *10* 79, *A Change of Seasons* 80, *Tarzan, The Ape Man* 81.

Bo Derek: her acting may leave something to be desired, but people flock to the theater to see her body.

Marlene Dietrich—who has been a screen goddess for 50 years.

Marlene Dietrich

Only legends are known by their last name and if Dietrich is not the foremost legendary film beauty of the century she is second only to Garbo. Hardly anyone in the whole world is known only by their first name but say Marlene and anyone anywhere will know who you mean. She made one of the finest and most famous movies of all time, *The Blue Angel*, 1930, and the image of her as a plump, not very blonde tart with good legs singing 'They Call Me Naughty Lola' is truly irresistible. In later movies her hair is so light it shimmers, her clothes are glamorous, and she gazes down at you from the screen with an icy intelligence behind which glows a smouldering mysterious eroticism.

For publicity shots she posed in cabaret costumes or swathed in boas. The most intriguing photographs show her in drag. In white or black tuxedo she projects a tough androgynous sexuality far more interesting and lucid than the vapid prettiness of so many movie stars. The same charisma comes through when she sings. The husky voice with the Elmer Fudd lisp conveys nostalgic memories of loves past and the promise of obsessive passion in the future. Never was there a movie vamp like the incomparable Marlene Dietrich.

She was born in 1901 in Schoneberg, a suburb of Berlin. Her given name was Maria Magdalene, later compressed into Marlene. Her father was an officer in the Royal Prussian Police Force, her mother's family were prominent jewellers. So her origins are middle-class.

Her father died when she was a baby and her mother remarried. Dietrich's step-father, Edouard von Losch, a Grenadier, was killed fighting in the First World War. His death left Dietrich, her mother and sister much poorer. But most German families were hurt in some way by the war.

Still Dietrich studied music, practicing the violin arduously, and dreaming of a career as a serious artist. When that dream proved unattainable in part due to muscle damage, Dietrich turned her attention to books. She devoured literature, and discovering she had a talent for reading poetry aloud, began to consider a career in theater. She auditioned for and was refused admittance to Max Reinhardt's Deutsches Theater. But she kept trying to break into acting and finally got her chance in a chorus line of a touring revue. Thus, a bit seasoned, she auditioned for Reinhardt's theater school again and this time she got in.

Germany in the 1920s was experiencing a cultural golden age. Reeling from defeat with all illusions destroyed, a hotbed of conflicting political ideologies, and seething with corruption and decadence, Germany nonetheless produced the greatest artists in Europe. This was true not only for painting and theater but for that newest of creative vehicles, film. From Max Reinhardt's theater school Dietrich learned the finest stage and lighting technique. Simultaneously, her work as an extra and bit player in films to earn a little money brought

Above: Dietrich in *Shanghai Express* (1932), as Shanghai Lil. The film concerned a train ride during a war in China.
Above right: Marlene Dietrich, the film goddess.

Below: Probably her most famous early role was as the night club entertainer, Lola-Lola, in *The Blue Angel* (1930), in which she introduced 'Falling in Love Again.'

Dietrich—beautiful, aloof, sophisticated, demanding, generous and world-weary. She also had beautiful legs.

her into contact with Berlin film makers at an exceedingly opportune moment.

But Dietrich, like many great stars, guarded her privacy by inventing her past. *The Blue Angel* was not her first film, though she later pretended it was and she was no mere acting student when she first came to von Sternberg's attention, another of her tales. Nor was she dancing in a revue, as he claimed. The truth is Dietrich made many movies in Germany. She even appeared in a crowd scene in one of Garbo's films. In 1923 she was in *Tragodie der Liebe/Tragedy of Love* with Emil Jannings playing a wrestler on trial and Dietrich the judge's mistress. There was nothing special about the part but the director Joe May sent his casting director to oversee auditions. The casting director was Rudolf Sieber. He not only chose Dietrich for the role, he married her in 1924.

Theirs was not a conventional marriage but its endurance reveals Dietrich's uniqueness. Though she's always remained her own person, living her life as she sees fit, she has integrity. Dietrich is loyal to those she

loves. When a daughter, Maria, was born in 1925, Dietrich proved an adoring mother. She remained devoted to Maria, even reserving judgment on working in Hollywood until she was sure California was a good place to raise kids. She was to make an equally ardent grandmother after Maria was grown and married.

Dietrich had a featured role in the 1926 *Manon Lescaut* and a small part in *Eine Du Barry von Heute/A Modern Du Barry*, 1928. Both films were released in America. She made a few comedies and thrillers, all on a shoestring budget, appeared in a starring role on stage in Vienna, returned to Reinhardt and got her first solo in one of his productions, then went on to co-star in several silent films. Her reputation as a stage actress was growing. She did Shakespeare and Shaw. That her movie roles were slight didn't phase her. She considered the theater her 'real' career and films simply a way of making money. Then came *The Blue Angel*, 1930, and so explosive a success could only change the course of her career and her life.

Director Josef von Sternberg was born into an im-

Above: Dietrich was not afraid to appear in cowboy films, such as *The Spoilers* (1942). Randolph Scott also starred. Her other suitor in the film was John Wayne.

Below: Dietrich, still glamorous in her seventies.

poverished Orthodox Jewish Austrian family. He was in his mid-30s when he picked Dietrich to star in an important film, one which was designed to introduce silent film actor Emil Jannings in a talking picture. A top director both in Germany and America, von Sternberg had literally clawed his way to the top, creating a legend of his own. He was a remarkable talent and he was anxious to find exactly the right vehicle for Jannings's transition to sound. He settled on a 1905 novel, Heinrich Mann's *Professor Unrath*, the story of a teacher punished by society for marrying a cabaret singer, who uses his wife as a source of revenge. It was 1929 and there was a whiff of Naziism in the air of Berlin. UFA Studios, where the film would be made, had been bought by a right-wing businessman. Since the movie with its sadism and cruelty was a comment on German society, von Sternberg showed a certain flamboyant courage in making the film.

However von Sternberg got hold of Dietrich, and the myths are many, she was obviously the perfect choice for *The Blue Angel*. As the detached little tart who humiliates the professor, she stole the picture and rose instantly into the firmament of top international stars. She even seemed to own the songs she sang. '*Falling In Love Again*' won applause from her audiences for decades afterwards.

Ironically, Dietrich had her doubts about the film, expecting it to hurt her career. Yet nothing she did thereafter ever equalled it, even though her next film *Morocco*, 1930, co-starring Gary Cooper, was an enormous smash. It was also something else. It was a Paramount film and that meant Hollywood. So Dietrich and von Sternberg came to America in 1930. After completing work on *Morocco* and again after her next movie *Dishonoured*, 1931, Dietrich returned to Berlin to be with her husband and child. By now she was a fabulous star in Germany, too, but strongly anti-Nazi. She could see where Germany was headed and got Sieber and Maria out in time. Her sister Elizabeth was less fortunate. She was sent to a concentration camp. Dietrich was Germany's most famous export and Hitler ordered her to return to Germany. When she refused, her movies were banned and she was accused of being 'unGerman' because of her many close friendships with Jews.

Dietrich's Hollywood allure was of a different order altogether than Lola-Lola's. She was a European and thus exotic to American audiences. On screen she was a woman of mystery and romance, ever more glamorous as the Depression deepened and movies purveyed wilder dreams of wealth. No actress knew more about lighting and cameras than Dietrich; no director had a greater sense of the fantastic than von Sternberg. As Shanghai Lilly in *Shanghai Express*, 1932, she was heart-breakingly beautiful. In the bizarre *Blonde Venus* of the same year she boldly stepped out of a gorilla costume. Few other glamorous stars would have dared it.

But Dietrich was different. When von Sternberg's

Dietrich shocked the world by appearing in men's clothing, but soon women were all wearing slacks.

wife sued her for alienation of affection, Dietrich fought back, against Paramount's advice, and won the case. She liked to wear slacks. Much to the horror of studio bigwigs she allowed herself to be photographed in them, and to their surprise started a national trend. When her friends were sick she'd bring them chicken soup and clean their houses. Beauty was useful to her, so was fame. But she always maintained an earthy Germanic level-headedness.

Dietrich made *The Song of Songs* with director Rouben Mamoulian in 1933, was a dazzlingly ornate Catherine The Great in *The Scarlet Empress*, 1934, again with von Sternberg, and was even more bejewelled in *The Devil Is A Woman*, 1935, her last film with von Sternberg. By now von Sternberg's baroque style had taken Dietrich as far as it could and it was time for her to show a cooler, more elegant, sparkling side.

Lubitsch produced and Borzage directed one of her greatest movies, *Desire*, 1936, with Gary Cooper. Von Sternberg's plots had been silly. But, like Grand Opera, audiences didn't go to see them for the story line. Visual image is what counted to von Sternberg but towards the end, despite the epic grandeur of his films, Dietrich is presented as simply his most lustrous ornament, the most glittering object on an over elaborate set.

In contrast, *Desire* had a darling bubble of a plot. Cooper was charming and boyish as the innocent American who runs into a sophisticated con-artist, Dietrich. She is human and appealing despite the glamor, and the film is a treat.

By now Dietrich was established as one of Hollywood's most highly paid luminaries no matter what, but she never became a Hollywood fixture. Though her husband was happy to withdraw to a California chicken farm, Dietrich never lost her cosmopolitanism. Her friends were international celebrities like Ernest Hemingway and Noel Coward. She couldn't be bothered spending her time social climbing with Hollywood's dull business-minded elite, like so many stars did, not even when her films began losing money and it would have been to her advantage to have an in with the right people.

During these dark days of the mid to late 30s one movie, *Angel*, in 1937, with Melvyn Douglas and Herbert Marshall, did her justice. It was a cinematic gem. But by now the critics were down on her no matter what she did. She was accused of not even bothering to act on screen, and she was getting older. Paramount lost interest in her.

Then in 1939 she did a Western comedy *Destry Rides Again* for Universal Pictures. It was a satire, co-starring James Stewart. She took a cut in salary to do it but it was just what she needed. It knocked her off her pedestal by showing the world she had a sense of humor and it put

Dietrich played a key role in *Witness for the Prosecution* (1958), Agatha Christie's courtroom drama.

her back on top of the star charts again. She was an American citizen by this time and her career shifted to a new theater, the theater of war.

No performer gave more to the war effort than Dietrich in the 1940s. In part because she was German, the symbolic meaning of her tours to entertain American GIs cannot be underestimated. She visited hospitals, lectured, helped with war bond drives, winning citizenship awards by the bundle. It was during World War II that she perfected her cabaret singing style, proving she didn't need a camera to be charismatic. Ever an original, she even played on a strange musical saw! Ah, Dietrich.

She played a German cabaret singer in *A Foreign Affair*, 1948. It was one of her best post-war films. She had a small but notable part in Hitchcock's *Stage Fright*, 1950, and played a movie star in the popular *No Highway*, 1951. She appeared in Orson Welles's interesting movie, *Touch of Evil*, 1958. Her strongest role during that time was in Agatha Christies's *Witness For The Prosecution*, 1958. In 1961 she did *Judgement at Nuremberg*.

But from the 50s on, Dietrich's interests spanned more than movies. She had a brief fling with radio, when she did a series called 'Café Istanbul.' She sang in cabaret in London and Las Vegas, pulling in pots of money and looking absolutely fantastic in dazzling costumes. She toured Germany. Though she met some protests there because of her pro-Allied stance during the War, she played to standing room only.

She made records. Her version of '*Where Have All The Flowers Gone?*' was one of the all-time best selling records in Europe. She did some European films but they were peripheral to her. She had found her new métier and in clubs she was magnetic. But then Dietrich had always taken live performances more seriously than filmed ones.

She is over 80 now and lives in Europe. During her long life she's known fame, wealth and adoration. So here's a toast: to Dietrich; to Marlene, one of the most extraordinary women of the 20th century.

Marlene Dietrich: *The Tragedy of Love* 23, *Manon Lescaut* 26, *A Modern du Barry* 28, *I Kiss Your Hand Madame* 29, *The Blue Angel* 30, *Morocco* 30, *Dishonoured* 31, *Shanghai Express* 32, *Blonde Venus* 32, *Song of Songs* 33, *The Scarlet Empress* 34, *The Devil Is a Woman* 35, *Desire* 36, *The Garden of Allah* 36, *Knight Without Armour* 37, *Angel* 37, *Destry Rides Again* 39, *Seven Sinners* 40, *The Flame of New Orleans* 41, *Manpower* 41, *The Lady is Willing* 42, *The Spoilers* 42, *Pittsburgh* 42, *Follow the Boys* 44, *Kismet* 44, *Martin Roumagnac* 46, *Golden Earrings* 47, *A Foreign Affair* 48, *Stage Fright* 50, *No Highway* 51, *Rancho Notorious* 52, *The Monte Carlo Story* 57, *Around the World in Eighty Days* 57, *Witness for the Prosecution* 58, *Touch of Evil* 58, *Judgement at Nuremberg* 61, *Paris When it Sizzles* 64, *Just a Gigolo* 78.

Greta Garbo

She is the supreme goddess of film. No one will ever equal her or replace her. Worshipped by the multitudes, idealized by intellectuals, she has been Hollywood's greatest legend for nearly 60 years. The name, Greta Garbo, has a magic to this day. Say it and what name equals it save Bernhardt's? No woman's beauty was ever praised more highly except possibly Helen of Troy's. She is loved worldwide. To the French she is 'La Divine.' To the Swedes she is a national treasure. To all of us she is simply Garbo, the finest fantasy the movies ever produced.

Somewhere back before the legend there was a baby born in 1905 who was christened Greta Lovisa Gustafsson. Her parents were poor though not destitute and lived in a small cold-water flat on the fourth floor of an apartment building in Stockholm. No miracles occurred during her childhood. There was no sign of what was to come. When she was 14 her father died and she had to quit school and get a job. She worked as a *tvalficka*, a soaplather girl, in a barbershop. She was plump, pretty, amiable and totally star-struck. She wanted to become an actress.

Greta managed to get a sales job in PUB, a Stockholm department store. Modeling hats for the store's catalogue led to an appearance in a PUB promotional film. Next came another brief film, this one advertising bakery goods for the Consumers' Cooperative Association of Stockholm. So far, this is scarcely a glamorous start for a legend. In 1922 a movie producer named Erik Petschler went shopping at PUB's. He had a couple of actresses with him whom Greta noticed. Chatting with them gave her the courage to phone Petschler later and ask for an interview. He cast her in a Mack Sennett type comedy called *Luffa-Petter/Peter the Tramp*, 1922. She and two other girls cavorted about in bathing suits. After that she was on her own.

So the future legend, committed more firmly than ever now to a career in the performing arts, knocked around Stockholm, getting poorer by the day and meeting little encouragement from movie producers. Running into Petschler again she was advised to try for a scholarship at the Royal Dramatic Theatre Academy, directing her to a talented and influential private coach. Greta was accepted, a rare honor and achievement. At school she worked hard but spoke little, perhaps because most of the students came from wealthier backgrounds than hers and had more social polish.

The Academy was a magnificent training ground for actors and what would have happened to Greta had she directed her interest towards the stage will never be known. Perhaps she would have been a star. Perhaps she would have remained a minor actress. It doesn't matter, because the so far prosaic story finally takes a miraculous twist. Carl Brisson was a popular music hall artist whom Greta, now 17, had a crush on. She tended to pester him and to get rid of her he recommended her to a director he knew, suggesting she might qualify for a part in his latest film, *The Atonement of Gösta Berling*, 1924. Greta arrived for a screen test, striking everyone around her as an ordinary young girl, except for one person. The director, Mauritz (Moje) Stiller, took one look at her and decided she would someday be the most beautiful movie star in the world. He fancied himself Pygmalion and set about finding the right name for his Galatea. He liked the ring of Mona Gabor, after the Hungarian king, Gabor Bethlen, but saying it over and over in different languages he hit upon a variation he liked better. Garbo.

She was everything he wanted her to be but it took time and the most amazing efforts on his part for the world to realize it. Colorful, rich, and famous as Stiller was, he devoted much of the remainder of his life to Garbo. She continued her studies at the Academy, occasionally going off with Stiller to make movies. He took her to Istanbul but money problems forced their return before they could finish the film they were working on there. They did better in Berlin where *Gösta Berling* got raves. Stiller let Garbo work with G W Pabst, but he guarded her jealously. Then in 1925 Stiller was approached by Louis B Mayer of MGM, always on the lookout for European talent. Stiller would not come to America without Garbo so, though Mayer wasn't very impressed with her, he signed them both.

It was the age of silent pictures, of flickering screens, bizarre plots, fantastic costuming. Movies were baroque fantasies, grand operas without sound. They provided an exotic escape to mainly unsophisticated audiences, and because the images on screen did not speak, facial expression was vitally important. Nobody's face was as expressive as Garbo's.

Yet, when she first reached California, nothing much happened. Garbo submitted to the usual phony cheesecake poses but Stiller got Arnold Genthe to take a marvelous photograph of Garbo that appeared in the magazine *Vanity Fair* and which helped convince the studio brass that Garbo was dazzlingly photogenic, dramatic, and mysterious. She was cast in *The Torrent*, which caused a crisis because Stiller was not allowed to direct it. Stiller and Garbo expected disaster but the 1926 movie was a big success. Stiller began directing her next film, *The Temptress*, also 1926, but he was removed from the picture. Life in Hollywood never agreed with Stiller. He tried working at Paramount, had problems there, grew ill, and went back to Sweden in 1928, where he died at the age of 45. It was a black day for Garbo. Although she'd struck out on her own by then, he'd remained a major force in her life.

Part of Stiller's legacy to Garbo was a distrust of Hollywood. To him it was a place to make money, not to express yourself artistically, a sleazy world of cheap publicity stunts where you'd be swallowed whole if you weren't careful. Garbo, who had taste, always fought for better parts and a higher salary. She had an easier time

Above: With John Gilbert in *A Woman of Affairs* (1929), a silent film about a reckless socialite.

Below: With Charles Bickford in *Anna Christie* (1930), the story of a woman with a shady past who loves a sailor.

Above: Garbo appeared again with John Gilbert in *Romance* (1930) as a tragic bad woman who is punished for her sins.

Below: John Barrymore was her co-star in *Grand Hotel* (1932), a film that has since become a classic.

gaining control of her income than her pictures. She was frequently cast as a seductive siren in melodramas that were not worthy of her, as she herself knew.

Perhaps distrust of the Hollywood studio system contributed to Garbo's dislike of publicity. Maybe it was her lack of English. Then again perhaps it was merely a natural reticence. Whatever, her attitude to the press was unique and the effect of seeking privacy brought her more attention than any other star. While others hurled themselves in front of cameras and chased reporters, Garbo ran the other way. She refused to sign autographs, pose for pictures or grant interviews. In public she frequently used an assumed name and wore wide-brimmed hats to disguise her appearance. She lived in seclusion, for a time even keeping her phone number a secret from the studio.

In 1927 Garbo and romantic lead John Gilbert literally drove America wild with *Flesh and the Devil*. After only three US films, Garbo was at the top of the Hollywood heap. It was rumored that Garbo and Gilbert had a real love affair going, and that certainly didn't hurt box office sales. Sick of playing the vamp, Garbo refused MGM's next choice of film for her. The studio tried to coerce her but they were up against something new, a star who wouldn't capitulate. Garbo meant it when she said she'd chuck Hollywood and go back to Sweden if they didn't give her what she wanted. She kept away from MGM for months, spending her time taking long walks, seeing the few people she liked and brooding. In the end she won her strike. Not only did MGM allow Garbo to play Anna Karenina in *Love*, 1927, but they raised her salary to the skies, making other important concessions as well. When it came to things financial the young woman from Sweden was turning into a very shrewd lady.

Garbo was not happy with the script of *Love* but with Gilbert playing Vronsky she did the part anyway and the picture garnered raves from the critics and dollars from the fans. Garbo was changing the style of women not only in America but in Europe as well. Women wore hats like Garbo's, copied her hair style, tried to look as if they, too, possessed what the Russians called 'soul.'

MGM decided Garbo should play Sarah Bernhardt. Though in the end the movie bore little resemblance to the great stage actress's life, *The Divine Woman*, 1928, showed Garbo's beauty off to great advantage. Garbo was a Russian spy in *The Mysterious Lady*, 1928. She co-starred with John Gilbert again in *A Woman of Affairs*, 1929, the film version of Michael Arlen's novel, *The Green Hat*. Critics were not as pleased with her in *Wild Orchids*, 1929, but her performance may have reflected her state of mind. Garbo had learned of Moje Stiller's death during the filming.

She returned to Sweden for a visit as soon as the film was made. Garbo had been homesick since her arrival in America anyway and she was especially eager to be with

Above: Garbo smiles at her husband (Basil Rathbone) while clutching her son (Freddie Bartholomew) in *Anna Karenina* (1935).

Below: She starred with Charles Boyer in *Conquest* (1938). He was Napoleon; she played the Countess Walewska.

her family at this time. She discovered that she was too monumental a star for her plaintive cry of 'I vant to be left alone' ever to be heard anywhere. Plagued by reporters on the ship, mobs pursued her in Stockholm. During the time at sea Garbo made the acquaintance of several of Sweden's wealthiest aristocrats. They were totally awed by her and flattered to know her. It didn't matter anymore that she was from a working-class district in Stockholm. She was Greta Garbo and the world was at her feet.

The Single Standard and *The Kiss*, both 1929, were silent movies, but the age of sound had arrived. Many stars, like John Gilbert with his high-pitched voice, would never survive the transition. The burning question at MGM was: would Garbo? In 1930 she made *Anna Christie*, in part because the Eugene O'Neill play features a character who could conceivably have a Swedish accent. Garbo made her entrance after the movie had run over a full half hour and breathed these immortal words, 'Gimme a visky. Chincher ale on the side. And don't be stingee, baybee.' Her husky voice passed muster. Critics cheered and MGM bosses relaxed.

The studio began to fall in line with Garbo and allow her privacy. Strangers were kept off the set when she was working. Little eccentricities like bringing her lunch to the studio in a paper bag every day were indulged. Of course the less the newspapers had of real news the more they spread stories about her. She was supposed to be tight-fisted, watching her pennies closely. She didn't care about glamorous clothes, preferring suits and men's ties. Plain oxfords were her favorite choice of shoe for the famous long and narrow Garbo feet. She went in for health foods, swimming, tennis and horseback riding. Garbo herself never bothered to deny or admit what she did and the fan magazines were free to speculate as they chose.

On the set Garbo was an industrious worker, a real pro. She had to be since MGM gave her very little time off. *Romance*, 1930, and *Inspiration*, 1931 were pictures in the usual mold. Garbo is the tragic bad woman who suffers for her sins. *Susan Lennox*, 1931, co-starring Clark Gable, offered more. It survives as one of her greatest films. She wanted to play George Bernard Shaw's Saint Joan and she got stuck with *Mata Hari* instead, 1932. She's the shining light in *Grand Hotel*, 1932 despite the competition from so many stars, and she won praise from Pirandello for the screen version of his *As You Desire Me*, 1932.

By now she had detractors, and her box office appeal was beginning to slide, but Garbo was Garbo, and MGM was willing to pay any price to keep her. Just to have her name on the studio's roster was the epitome of prestige. Garbo had become intrigued with the idea of doing a picture based on the life of Queen Christina of Sweden, an interesting historical character who refused to marry, took lovers as she pleased and wore men's clothes.

Garbo played a dual role in her last film, *Two Faced Woman* (1941). Here she dances the 'Chica-Choca.'

A studio publicity portrait of Greta Garbo in one of her more outlandish costumes.

Rouben Mamoulian directed it, using close-ups of the beautiful face to achieve the effect he wanted. *Queen Christina*, 1933, was an outstanding film, hugely popular abroad, where the interest in Garbo never slackened.

The Painted Veil, 1934, came next, followed by *Anna Karenina*, 1935, which won her the New York Critics Best Actress Award, and *Camille*, which earned her an Oscar nomination, her first. It is perhaps her most highly respected film. *Conquest*, a lavish movie with Charles Boyer as Napoleon, 1938, created less interest than Garbo's trip to Europe with conductor Leopold Stokow-

ski. The pair were besieged by reporters, snatching privacy as best they could. Gossip columnists ruminated over whether the divorced Stokowski would marry the enigmatic Garbo but in reality they had no idea whether the relationship was romantic or platonic. When the vacation was over, Garbo came back alone, startling reporters by granting them an interview. It proved totally uninformative. The star returned to California to make her one great comedy, *Ninotchka*, 1939.

If Garbo hadn't died a thousand deaths it's only because she hadn't made a thousand films. The beauty of her sensitive face and her genius for tragedy meant that she was usually cast as a desperate and dangerous woman. In Hollywood movies of her era such women either died or met an end so bleak that death would have seemed a cheerful alternative. Garbo had been funny in *Peter The Tramp* but not since that early romp had she been allowed to do comedy. *Ninotchka*, the story of a Russian Revolutionary whom love and glamor win over to the west, was delightful. Lubitsch directed, Melvyn Douglas co-starred. When Garbo laughed she was so terrific the world literally laughed with her. She was nominated for an Academy Award again, but still didn't get it.

About this time Garbo became interested in the dietetic theories of Gaylord Hauser. Again, the gossip mills got busy but the relationship between Garbo and Hauser appears to have been strictly one of student to mentor. World War II cut Garbo off from her European market, a serious loss, and the Hays office landed on her movie, *Two Faced Woman*, 1941, forcing revisions which undercut the film's lightness and humor. The National Legion of Decency attacked the movie, too, and the Catholic Interest Committee of the Knights of Columbus of Manhattan and the Bronx denounced it. *Two Faced Woman* was a mild farce, with a bit of sexual intrigue. A decade earlier no one would have been shocked by it. The movie represented a change for Garbo. She revealed a new coquettish side of herself, but MGM's tampering to please the censors did the film in, and stripping Garbo of glamor did not sit well except with her most ardent fans.

It was her last movie. She was only 36 but she retired from films, though no one can be sure whether she meant to leave the screen permanently at the time. There was talk of her making a movie after World War II but nothing ever came of it. She continued to lead a highly private life, alternating her time between Europe and New York. Though she tried to hide her identity or go unnoticed, Garbo-spotting became a great pastime. Just to catch a glimpse of her was somehow a feather in one's cap.

Today Garbo's appeal is stronger than ever and even the young are captivated by her beauty and talent on screen. If all other legends fade, surely hers will endure, for Garbo is Hollywood's immortal goddess.

Greta Garbo: *Peter the Tramp* 22, *The Atonement of Gösta Berling* 24, *Joyless Street* 25, *The Torrent* 26, *The Temptress* 26, *Flesh and the Devil* 27, *Love* 27, *The Mysterious Lady* 28, *The Divine Woman* 28, *The Kiss* 29, *A Woman of Affairs* 29, *Wild Orchids* 29, *The Single Standard* 29, *Anna Christie* 30, *Romance* 30, *Inspiration* 31, *Susan Lennox* 31, *Mata Hari* 32, *Grand Hotel* 32, *As You Desire Me* 32, *Queen Christina* 33, *The Painted Veil* 34, *Anna Karenina* 35, *Camille* 36, *Conquest* 38, *Ninotchka* 39, *Two Faced Woman* 41.

Above: Garbo's co-star in *Camille* (1936) was Robert Taylor, who played Camille's lover, Armand.

Below: Garbo played the famous World War I female spy in *Mata Hari* (1932), with Ramon Novarro.

The gorgeous Betty Grable in a scene from *My Blue Heaven* (1950), in which she played a radio star.

Betty Grable

There was nothing pale and silvery about her. She came packaged in technicolor, an on-screen sunburst of yellow hair, red lips and rosy fleshtones. Musicals were her métier. The public loved to watch Betty Grable in vivid and elaborate costumes sing and dance her way through a make-believe turn-of-the-century world. Though she had fabulous legs she wasn't unobtainably beautiful or too glamorous to believe in. A guy could dream of meeting a girl like Betty Grable in a war plant, at a diner, or at the USO. No wonder she was GI Joe's favorite blonde.

Unlike most stars, Betty Grable on screen wasn't too different from Betty Grable for real. She was generous, she was nice, and she was modest. Born in St Louis in 1916, Ruth Elizabeth Grable was the kind of ordinary kid who if left alone might never have considered a career in show business. But Betty's mother Lillian was a real stage mama. Having failed to make a dancer or singer out of her oldest daughter Marjorie, Lillian took a firm hold on the more pliable Betty. At four Betty took toe, ballet, tap and acrobatics. Saxophone, ukelele and trap drums came next. Mama pushed her into talent shows when she was only seven. When Betty balked, her mother, who was prevented from being a performer herself in part because of an injured hip, would do everything in her power to bring Betty back to her senses. Usually, the simple reminder that Betty's birth had aggravated Lillian's hip condition did the trick.

Betty's father Conn Grable (possibly changed from Grasle) was a stockbroker, a successful self-made man until the Depression of the 1930s knocked his career flat. While he still had money he could afford to give Betty a brief spin at a fancy girl's school, Mary Institute. But when a visiting talent scout said Betty belonged in Hollywood, her future was settled. Conn stayed in St Louis but Lillian and 12-year-old Betty moved to California. Through all the tough times ahead while Betty tried to make it big in pictures, Conn faithfully sent his wife and child enough money to live on.

Betty was only 14 when she was chosen to be in the chorus line in *Let's Go Places*, 1930. She looked older but Fox dropped her contract when the studio learned her true age. Next she became a Goldwyn girl and appeared in *Whoopee*, 1930, which starred Eddie Cantor. She made educational shorts, was picked up by RKO when Goldwyn dropped her, went on tour with Frank Fay and Barbara Stanwyck in *Tattle Tales*, sang with Ted Florito and his band and had a bright moment in the Fred Astaire Ginger Rogers hit, *The Gay Divorcee*, 1934, singing 'Let's Knock Knees' with Edward Everett Horton. Now came the Betty co-ed era with Betty playing a student in the kind of light-hearted low-budget college movies the studios loved to put their starlets in. *Old Man Rhythm*, 1935, Paramount's *Collegiate*, 1936, 20th Century Fox's *Pigskin Parade*, 1936 are examples of the breed.

So far Betty had bounced around, gaining experience

Above: Betty Grable was one of the most popular musical comedy stars of the 1940s.

Below: Grable often starred in musical films with John Payne—a general purpose leading man.

but igniting no fires. She even tried a name change for a while calling herself Francis Dean. But she went back to Betty Grable. She was to appear in close to 30 movies before she achieved stardom. Granted stardom is rare under any circumstances but part of the problem may have been her age. She was simply too young to project the kind of sexiness demanded of her and her singing and dancing were not spectacular enough to win her fame on talent alone.

Then came Betty's big break, but it happened off-screen, not on. In the summer of 1935 Betty and Mama Lillian were on a day cruise to Catalina when former child star Jackie Coogan introduced himself to them. Betty had caught the eye of George Raft and he was to notice her again later but Lillian had strictly limited Betty's social life so far.

Coogan had a lot more to offer than Raft or anyone else Betty had met. Like Raft he was famous. Unlike Raft he was young. He was also presumably about to inherit a fortune, based on his childhood earnings. Unfortunately for Betty and Jackie that was not to be. His mother and stepfather had acquired full control of his wealth and a legal battle followed, ultimately leading to the adoption of the Coogan law to guarantee that child actors would receive a significant part of their earnings when they grew up.

But all that lay ahead when Betty started dating Jackie. There were no clouds on his horizon as far as anyone knew and he was one of Hollywood's most desirable bachelors. By December Betty was off on a nation-wide tour with him in a vaudeville show called *Hollywood Secrets*. They got a lot of publicity. The couple were married in 1937. Betty got a good part in Paramount's *This Way Please*, 1937, with Jack Benny and Mary Livingstone. She was shown off with Coogan in *College Swing*, 1938. *Campus Confessions*, 1938, gave her top billing for the first time, and *Million Dollar Legs*, 1939, had her a cheer leader, again with Jackie as co-star. The legs are a football team's, not Grables, though hers would one day be worth as much.

Betty's marriage to Jackie Coogan was beset with money problems, youthful immaturities and in-law problems on both sides. They stayed together a year and eight months, Betty's divorce coinciding with her parents'. After 30 years Conn and Lillian decided to part for good.

Though Betty's personal life contained divorce, in her professional life she was about to meet her mate. In 1935 Darryl F Zanuck took over the Fox studio and merged it with his own 20th Century. He signed Betty, in a sense bringing her back to the place she'd begun when she danced for Fox in *Let's Go Places*, her first film. This marriage would last a long time and be highly lucrative. Zanuck allowed her to do a featured role in *Du Barry Was A Lady*, a Cole Porter musical that starred Ethel Merman and Bert Lahr.

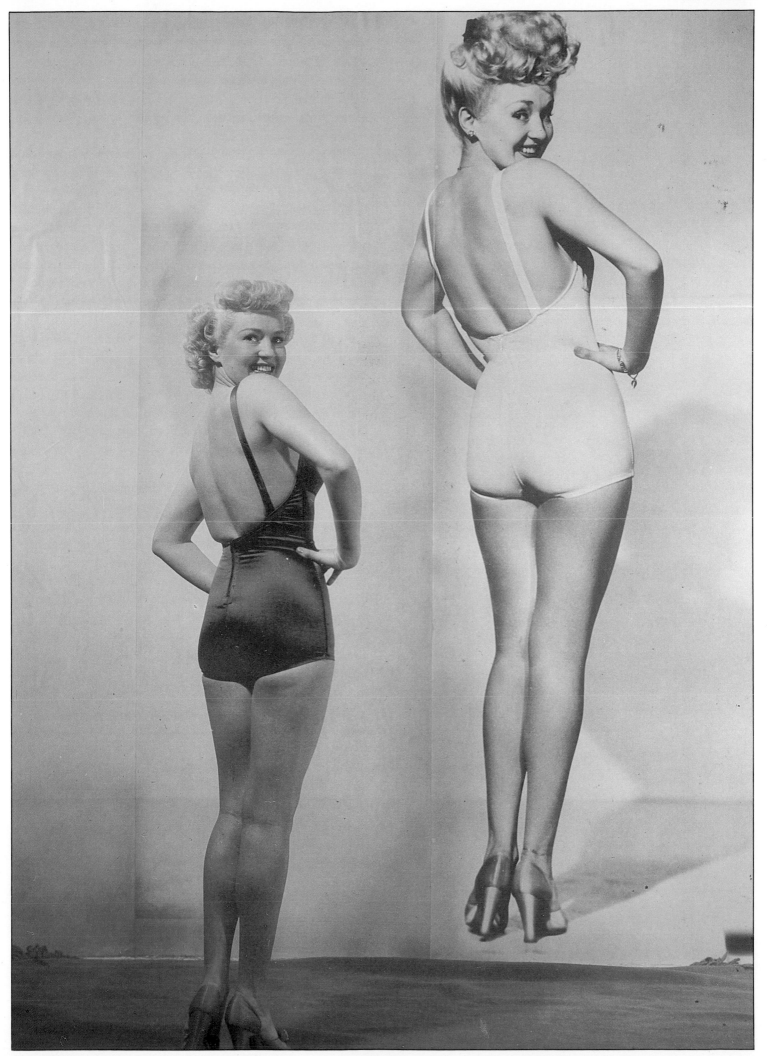

Grable and the pin-up picture that hung in millions of Army lockers during World War II. 'My legs made me,' she said.

Above: Robert Cummings tries to romance Grable as Don Ameche looks on in *Moon Over Miami* (1941).

Below: Grable (left) and June Haver played *The Dolly Sisters* (1946)—a film about the vaudeville sister team.

New York liked Betty. She was always to be popular there even after she returned to the screen. On stage Betty danced, sang and looked good in costumes. Offstage she found a new romantic interest, band leader Artie Shaw, until he surprised her and everyone else by a love-at-first-sight elopement with Lana Turner in California.

Betty was on tour with *Du Barry* when Zanuck pulled her out to replace an ailing Alice Faye in the movie that would at last put Betty at the very top. The movie was called *Down Argentine Way*, 1940. The movie was in color and color was what Betty had always needed. She and co-star Don Ameche clicked on film. The movie was supposed to appeal to South American audiences, for war had cut off the lucrative European market. Appropriately, the Brazilian Bombshell, Carmen Miranda, was also in the film.

More musicals and straight films followed for Betty until the Japanese attack on Pearl Harbor on 7 December 1941 assured America's entrance into the war. Betty's career zoomed. By 1942 Betty Grable was one of Hollywood's top ten stars and the era of the Second World War proved to be her peak period of fame. The reason is simple. She had just what was needed to be America's number one pin-up girl.

There was always a wholesomeness about Betty which never turned treacly, and a vulgarity that added spice to the family fare she appeared in. That meant the Hays Office and the women's clubs were happy with her, yet the boys at the front were free to find her sexy. Betty reveled in the glory of stardom. She threw a lot of good parties, but then Betty always knew how to have fun. A zenith of sorts was reached when her legs were insured with Lloyds of London for an even higher amount than Fred Astaire's. She left her thigh prints in the cement at Grauman's Chinese Theatre in 1943, the same year she married famous trumpet player Harry James.

Her pictures were basically alike. In *Song of the Islands*, 1942, Betty wore a grass skirt and sang to Victor Mature. *Coney Island*, 1943, revealed her as a showgirl in a much sanitized carnival world. *Sweet Rosie O'Grady*, 1943, showed Betty as a Brooklyn singer who makes it very big in London. *Pin-Up Girl*, 1944, had Betty playing a secretary who sends pin-up photos to GIs. Hermes Pan did the choreography. *Billy Rose's Diamond Horseshoe*, 1945, and *The Dolly Sisters*, 1946, continued the song and dance tradition.

By 1946 Betty was the highest-paid American woman. She and Harry James owned a racing stable, ranches and two estates. She liked to gamble and so did he. Never burdened with excessive drive or a voracious ego, she often talked about retiring from movies and just enjoying life. But gambling losses and problems with the Internal Revenue Service made this choice impossible.

One of her best movies came after the war. *Mother Wore Tights*, 1947, cast her with Dan Dailey. They were

Rita Hayworth

She projected grace and sensuality, a rare combination in a Hollywood era where blondes with a knack for comedy usually emerged as sex symbols. With her glorious red hair spilling over her shoulders she literally made an entrance on film, technicolor's dream girl, tall, mysterious, the reigning beauty of her decade, the 1940s.

Margarita Carmen Cansino was her real name and she was born in 1918. Her father was a successful Spanish dancer in vaudeville, her mother had appeared in the Ziegfeld Follies. Margarita was expected to learn how to dance and she did, but she was never a stagestruck exhibitionist. Quiet, shy and sensitive, she performed because it was quite literally her family's stock in trade.

Lured to California by the burgeoning movie industry of the 1920s, the Cansinos quit New York and Margarita's father opened a dance studio. The 1930s Depression forced him to rejuvenate his dance act, this time with his daughter, not his wife, as partner. Margarita was scarcely in her teens, an incipient beauty who looked older. Her hair was very dark, she wore Spanish costumes, and performed mainly south of the border because Mexico's laws re working minors were loose. During this stint for survival on gambling boats and in night clubs, Margarita was strictly guarded by her parents. It was a grueling schedule and an unglamorous life but she learned some valuable lessons about work. In later years when she was Rita Hayworth, she was prompt, punctual, and co-operative. No phony playing the big star for her.

The Cansinos had always had some feedback to films since their arrival in California so it was only a small step from dancing in a club to dancing on screen for Margarita. With a push from her father, Margarita pulled in a little cash as an extra in crowd scenes. At last a contract with Fox was forthcoming, partly because unassuming and shy as she was, Margarita was splendidly photogenic. She had a prominent dance number with a partner in *Dante's Inferno*, 1935. The film was bad but she was good and got some attention. She had her first real scene in *Under the Pampas Moon*, 1935, as a Latin señorita. A bit part, but it was a beginning. That same year saw *Charlie Chan in Egypt*, and *Paddy O'Day* which starred Jane Withers.

Fox was now part of 20th Century Fox when *Human Cargo* was shot in 1936. By now she was Rita, not Margarita. Her roles were getting bigger, her billing better. But she was not yet a star and because of studio in-fighting was dropped by 20th Century Fox, then free-lanced a while before being picked up by Columbia Pictures, where she would ultimately become their hottest property.

She appeared in a series of 'B' pictures but this allowed the still uncertain though now more ambitious young girl a chance to learn the ropes. She took acting and voice lessons, slimmed down, and developed more style. Her career was helped along at this time by her agent and soon-to-be husband, Eddie Judson. He took care of the

Above: Rita Hayworth was truly a beauty.

Below: Born Margarita Carmen Cansino of Latin and Irish ancestry, Hayworth often played tempestuous roles. One of them was in *The Loves of Carmen* (1948).

business side of things: publicity, promotion, contracts. Taking the name Hayworth, a variation of her mother's maiden name, she had big parts in a string of formula films, consisting of Westerns, teen-aged pics, and one break away movie, *Only Angels Have Wings* in 1939. The film starred Jean Arthur and Cary Grant but Rita's entrance in a silver gray jersey had that scene-stealing sizzle.

Two more movies, *The Lady in Question,* her first appearance opposite Glenn Ford, and Ben Hecht's *Angels Over Broadway,* both 1940, were shadows of things to come. For Warner's *The Strawberry Blonde,* 1941, Rita got her really red hair, even though the film was shot in black and white. The movie was a lovely little piece of Hollywood turn of the century fluff and it put Rita on the map.

It was this slow steady proletarian route to the top that brought derision from the Hollywood back stabbers. Rita was nothing but a studio creation. Any kid on the block could have done it, just give her enough promotional treatment. Even the long painful process Rita endured to have her hair line changed gave them ammunition. What the gossips forgot, of course, was the number of girls churned out by the studios who went nowhere because they didn't have that ruby glow on the screen. There was more than a little prejudice in the remarks of many of her jealous detractors, who lumped Spain and Mexico into one big stereotype. They would have liked Rita better if she'd kept her fan and castanets.

Audiences liked Rita. They're the ones who made her a star, perhaps because she had a versatile appeal. She could play the good girl who gets the guy in a musical, as she did opposite Fred Astaire in such films as *You'll Never Get Rich,* 1941 and *You Were Never Lovelier,* 1942. She was a smash with Gene Kelly in *Cover Girl,* 1944. But she could also play the part of the wicked seductress. This she did so well she earned the title 'The Love Goddess,' and so became the idol of many a GI Joe during World War II.

Blood and Sand, 1941, first revealed this love goddess side. The movie was Spanish in feel, the color magnificent. Rita's seduction of Tyrone Power launched her to superstar status and when *Life* magazine did a spread on her the head of Columbia Pictures, Harry Cohn, realized at last he'd picked a winner. Columbia, which started small and started poor, had never been in the same league as Warner's or MGM, when it came to full-fledged stars.

In private life Rita was hitting the columns with her latest love, Hollywood's boy wonder and genius, Orson Welles. She divorced her first husband in 1942, marrying Orson in 1943. He brought something new into her life, the glitter of a brainy intellectual set. Surprisingly, despite box office hits and prestige openings at the high status Radio City Music Hall, Rita was still shy and relatively unworldly. Most of her time had been spent on a Hollywood set, working conscientiously, sometimes as long as 18 hours per day. Although a prized possession of the studio and exploited accordingly, she wasn't given any fancy treatment. It wasn't 'Miss Hayworth,' it was simply 'Rita' at Columbia. Whatever doors Orson Welles opened in Rita Hayworth's life, the man who terrified America with a radio adaptation of *The War of the Worlds* in 1938, and impressed America with the movie *Citizen Kane* in 1941, was a complex gregarious person. He liked to surround himself with people. Rita preferred privacy. It was a mismatch. The couple had one child, a daughter, Rebecca, when Rita announced that she was filing for divorce in 1945. Though she and Orson tried several reconciliations they didn't work.

Before they separated Orson had directed and co-starred with Rita in a film called *The Lady From Shanghai* which wasn't released until 1948. For this one film Rita's hair was cropped and she became a blonde. Since Rita then used her hair to create effects that other actresses today use their entire unclothed body to achieve, the long tresses were back for what was to be her super blockbuster, *Gilda*.

Released in 1946, *Gilda* was a post-war movie in every sense of the term. The prudery and sticky sweetness of late depression and World War II films was wearing off.

Above: The splendidly voluptuous Rita Hayworth.

Below: Hayworth starred with Frank Sinatra in *Pal Joey* (1957). She and another screen goddess, Kim Novak, battled over Sinatra, who played the heel-hero.

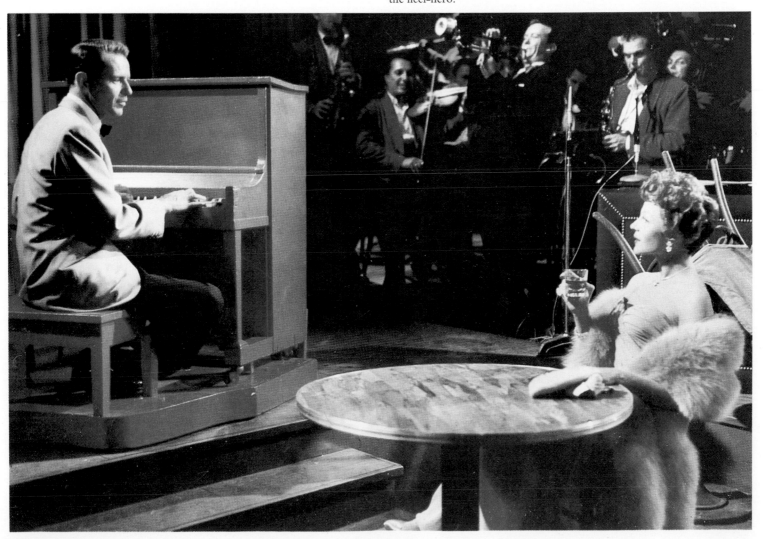

Above: Hayworth starred with Gene Kelly in *Cover Girl* (1944). She was a chorus girl who won fame and fortune.

Gilda was about a powerful love-hate relationship, with hints of sadism, masochism and homosexuality around the edges. Charlie Vidor was the director, Glenn Ford, back from military service and looking a lot more grown up for it, was the male lead. Though the movie's ending is a form of appeasement to the Hays office, it doesn't matter. The sex was there in the subtle alluring manner Rita generated. It was also there in Glenn Ford's reaction to her. When these two went into a clinch it was enough to give an audience hot chills.

Though Rita's voice was dubbed as usual when she sang 'Put the Blame on Mame,' the voice suits. Wearing a lustrous black strapless gown, Rita's bump and grind dance culminates in stripping off her long gloves and asking the ogling crowd to help her with the zipper. It's one of Hollywood's stand-out famous scenes. *Gilda* was such a success it initiated the whole line of Noir films, movies that revealed the seedy dark side of life.

As a real goddess in *Down To Earth* in 1947 and a sex symbol again in *The Loves of Carmen* a year later, Rita continued to be a box office draw. But something happened to Rita Hayworth that got more publicity than her films. In 1948 the saga of her romance with Aly Khan began.

They met in the South of France. He was rich as Midas, or rather as rich as his father, the Aga Khan, spiritual leader of the Ismaili Moslems, permitted him to be.

Separated from his English upper-class wife, Aly Khan was known in cafe society for his charm, his extravagance and his insatiable appetite for beautiful women. Until he met Rita he had been able to keep some lid on the press but she was far too famous for secrecy to succeed and their relationship became headline news. Theirs was the first great post-war scandal. Others, such as Ingrid Bergman's and Roberto Rossellini's, would follow.

Rita literally went dashing about Europe, accompanied by Aly, with reporters in fiery pursuit. Aly got a divorce. Rumors flew that Rita was pregnant. Back home in the USA the guardians of the pillars of morality were howling for Rita's head, particularly because she kept Rebecca with her. Rita's devotion was misinterpreted as neglect. But many of her fans were delighted with the whole affair, probably because *Gilda* had established Rita as a wicked woman rather than a saccharin sweetheart. Movie audiences had a tendency to confuse a star's film image with her private essence.

Their wedding in France was truly an Arabian Nights event. What with dazzling presents—diamonds, gold, cars, the works—it might have been filmed by Cecil B De Mille. The guest list glittered. Rita's clothes were divine. Her blue wedding dress was copied and put on sale at Macy's. But Aly wasn't one to give up the girls, and their fishbowl life was too much for Rita. The marriage lasted two years.

When Rita returned to America in 1951 she had a second child, daughter Yasmin, in tow. She made more movies but Hollywood was a different place. Television had come along and Tinseltown was in crisis. Among her films, *Miss Sadie Thompson*, 1953, showed she could still flash that old sexual magic. *Pal Joey* with Columbia's new star, Kim Novak, 1957, and *Separate Tables*, 1958, showed her off to advantage.

But something seemed to have happened to Rita. She'd always sparked to life before a camera. Now she was sometimes dull. A stormy marriage to Dick Haymes, who was involved in his own alimony struggles at the time, ended in divorce. She was married again to James Hill, a producer. They divorced in 1961. Rita, never an egomaniac, made a series of unglamorous 'B' movies. But her record as an unspoiled worker suffered. Sometimes she couldn't even remember her lines. Plans for her to appear in *Applause*, Lauren Bacall's big Broadway hit, fell through.

Tragically, her problem was misdiagnosed as alcoholism. Only recently has her true illness been recognized. Rita is a victim of Alzheimer's Disease which results in premature aging. Her case has done much to publicize the disease and her daughter Yasmin works actively to promote medical research. At the present time there is no cure for the disease.

Rita, a shell of her former self, lives in a New York apartment and receives 24-hour-a-day nursing care. Despite the sadness of the end of her story on screen her youthful image is undiminished. Tall and glamorous she is the crowning glory of Hollywood's fabulous 40s beauty queens.

Above: In *The Lady From Shanghai* (1948), Hayworth was directed by Orson Welles, who was then her husband.

Below: Hayworth played opposite Glenn Ford in *Gilda* (1946).

Rita Hayworth: *Dante's Inferno* 35, *Under the Pampas Moon* 35, *Charlie Chan in Egypt* 35, *Paddy O'Day* 35, *Human Cargo* 36, *Rebellion* 36, *Old Louisiana* 37, *Hit the Saddle* 37, *Trouble in Texas* 37, *Criminals of the Air* 37, *Girls Can Play* 37, *The Game That Kills* 37, *Paid to Dance* 37, *The Shadow* 37, *Who Killed Gail Preston?* 38, *There's Always a Woman* 38, *Convicted* 38, *Juvenile Court* 38, *Homicide Bureau* 38, *The Lone Wolf's Spy Hunt* 39, *Renegade Ranger* 39, *Only Angels Have Wings* 39, *Special Inspector* 39, *Music in My Heart* 40, *Blondie on a Budget* 40, *Susan and God* 40, *The Lady in Question* 40, *Angels Over Broadway* 40, *The Strawberry Blonde* 41, *Affectionately Yours* 41, *Blood and Sand* 41, *You'll Never Get Rich* 41, *My Gal Sal* 42, *Tales of Manhattan* 42, *You Were Never Lovelier* 42, *Cover Girl* 44, *Tonight and Every Night* 45, *Gilda* 46, *Down to Earth* 47, *The Lady from Shanghai* 48, *The Loves of Carmen* 48, *Affair in Trinidad* 52, *Salome* 53, *Miss Sadie Thompson* 53, *Fire Down Below* 57, *Pal Joey* 57, *Separate Tables* 58, *They Came to Cordura* 59, *The Story on Page One* 59, *The Happy Thieves* 62, *Circus World* 64, *The Money Trap* 66, *The Poppy is Also a Flower* 67, *The Rover* 67, *Sons of Satan* 68, *The Road to Salina* 70, *The Wrath of God* 72.

Audrey Hepburn, the gamin-faced screen goddess. Her charm is that she is proper without being stiff.

Audrey Hepburn

Film legend has it that the French author Colette spotted Audrey Hepburn in a hotel lobby in Monte Carlo and decided on the spot that she would be perfect for the leading role in the stage adaptation of her novel *Gigi*.

That story isn't quite at the level of the apocryphal tale of Lana Turner and Schwab's drugstore. Before *Gigi* Audrey was already a working actress and dancer. She had minor (sometimes very minor) parts in several films. But she was struggling. *Gigi* was the turning point for Audrey Hepburn's career.

Audrey Hepburn was born in Brussels in 1929 of Irish–Dutch parentage. She spent the war years in Belgium, and difficult and often hungry years they were. After the war she went to England to complete her education and to study ballet, for early in her career she was primarily a dancer. But she was also able to pick up bit parts in a number of continental and British movies. In the comedy classic *The Lavender Hill Mob*, 1951, she appears briefly as the girl who speaks to Alec Guiness at the end of the film.

Even at this early stage in her career Audrey had some enthusiastic backers among film people. She was beginning to be noticed. Her parts were getting bigger. But it wasn't until *Gigi* that her career really took off.

On her way to Broadway Audrey stopped off in London to take a screen test for Paramount. When director William Wyler saw the test he demanded her

for the lead in *Roman Holiday*, 1953. His original choice for the part, Jean Simmons, had backed out. The film was actually made during a summer recess in the Broadway run of *Gigi*. Ironically, Audrey Hepburn never played Gigi on the screen. That part went to another European dancer, Leslie Caron.

Roman Holiday was a light romantic comedy in which Audrey plays a modern princess who falls in love with an American newsman, Gregory Peck, while she is on an official visit to Rome. Everyone who saw the rushes knew that the film was going to be a hit and Audrey Hepburn would be a star. The public responded enthusiastically to the wispy, girlish, yet elegant Audrey. She also won a flock of awards for the film, including the Oscar for best actress.

What was her appeal? She was certainly no sex goddess like Marilyn Monroe whose career was also taking off at about this time. She had the body of a ballet dancer and an unusual and not conventionally pretty face. The cynical director Billy Wilder may have put his finger on the reason when he observed, 'After so many drive-in waitresses in movies—it has been a real drought—here is a class somebody who went to school, can spell, and possibly play the piano.' One starring role and Audrey was already being compared to Garbo, Ingrid Bergman and, of course, that other Hepburn, Katharine. She certainly had class.

It was Billy Wilder who directed her next film

Hepburn, as Natasha, dances with her then husband, Mel Ferrer, as Prince Andre, in *War and Peace* (1956).

Sabrina, 1954, in which she starred opposite two screen legends, Humphrey Bogart and William Holden. The film lacked the fluffy charm of *Roman Holiday*, but it confirmed Audrey's place as one of the most appealing new stars of the 1950s.

She went back to Broadway to star as a nymph in Giraudoux's *Ondine*. Her co-star was Mel Ferrer and they married at the end of the run. Ferrer played Prince Andre to Audrey's Natasha in *War and Peace*, 1956. The film was more traditional Hollywood historical epic than Tolstoy, but it was certainly no artistic disaster, and for many critics and much of the movie going public Audrey Hepburn *was* Natasha Rostov.

Next it was on to musical comedy, a revamp of the old Gershwin show *Funny Face*, 1957. Audrey's co-star was Fred Astaire, who declared himself eager to work with the youngster before he got too old.

Audrey's individualistic speaking voice had always been one of her greatest assets, and in this film she demonstrated a pleasant, if unspectacular, singing voice as well.

Over the next few years Audrey Hepburn had other successes, like *The Nun's Story*, 1959, which has been described as the best-ever American film dealing with religion. Author Truman Capote didn't like the film

version of his *Breakfast at Tiffany's*, 1961, which he described as 'a mawkish valentine to Audrey Hepburn.' But the public liked it very much indeed. There were also failures like *Green Mansions*, 1959 and *The Children's Hour*, 1962. Somehow Audrey's career seemed to be stalled. It was becoming apparent that while her sophisticated charm had great appeal in the large cities of America, and in much of Europe, her films weren't grabbing mass audiences in the great American heartland.

All that was supposed to change, for she had been given the role of Eliza in the screen version of *My Fair Lady*, 1964, at the time the most popular musical ever to hit Broadway. This was the best role in the biggest film to come along in years. It should have been a high point in Audrey's career. Yet it didn't quite work out that way. Yes, the film was a success artistically and financially, and, yes, she was lovely as Eliza. But she had been given the part over the popular Julie Andrews who had originated it on Broadway. The switch resulted in a lot of negative publicity for Audrey—the first she had ever gotten in her career. She was the big money star stealing the part from the talented newcomer. Julie Andrews in the meantime went on to do *Mary Poppins*, a film that did a lot more for her than *My Fair Lady* did for Audrey. The studio

Above: Hepburn and Peter O'Toole case a Paris museum to plot the crime in *How To Steal a Million* (1966).

Below: Dressed for Ascot in *My Fair Lady* (1964).

Below: As *Sabrina* (1954)—the chauffeur's daughter.

Above: Hepburn starred with Fred Astaire in *Funny Face* (1957).

Below: Hepburn appeared with George Peppard in *Breakfast at Tiffany's* (1961). She was a playgirl; he was a writer.

Below: Hepburn and Ben Gazzara in *Sidney Sheldon's Bloodline* (1977), in which she found her life endangered after inheriting a Zurich pharmaceutical company.

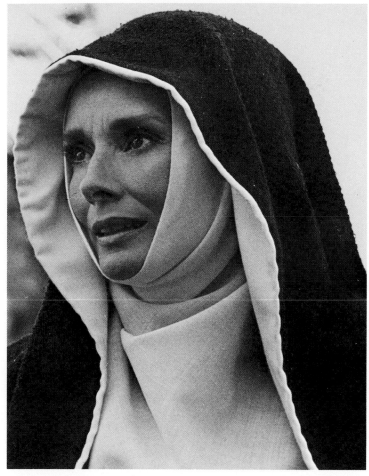

Above: She played an older Maid Marian in *Robin and Marian* (1976), in which she meets middle-aged Robin Hood again.

Below: In *Wait Until Dark* (1967), she was a blind woman.

biggies also decided that while Audrey had a pleasant enough singing voice, it just wasn't powerful enough for Eliza, so they dubbed her—more negative publicity. People whispered that they wouldn't have had to dub Julie Andrews. All in all *My Fair Lady* was a bit of a downer for Audrey.

Audrey kept making movies, usually very good ones. She scored a major critical success in *Two For the Road*, 1967, with Albert Finney, and she was very effective as the terrified blind girl in the chiller *Wait Until Dark*, 1967. But there were no more Garbo and Ingrid Bergman comparisons.

Audrey's marriage to Mel Ferrer ended in 1968 and the following year she married an Italian psychiatrist. Unlike many film stars Audrey Hepburn had never lived her personal life in public. And while her greatest successes had been in Hollywood films she had remained basically a European and she spent most of her time in either Switzerland or Italy. After her second marriage she announced that she regarded her career dangerous for her marriage and that she would make no more films, unless they could be made practically in her own back-yard.

Audrey hasn't quite lived up to that pledge, though she is known to have turned down several potentially juicy roles because they would have kept her away from home for too long. But Audrey was tempted out of her semi-retirement to make *Robin and Marion*, 1976, a wonderful and insufficiently appreciated film. She plays Maid Marion to Sean Connery's Robin Hood, in a tale of what happened to these two mythical lovers 20 years after. It was the first time she played an 'older woman' but she didn't look it. Audrey Hepburn fans were delighted to see that at nearly 50 she was still lovely and appealing. Three years later she returned again in *Bloodline*, 1979, an awful film—but she was still lovely. The following year she was back again in *They All Laughed*, director Peter Bogdonavich's unsuccessful attempt to put his own career back on track.

While Audrey Hepburn, either through choice or chance, never attained the sort of mythic status that she once seemed destined for, she added more than a touch of class to an era of film history in which class was generally lacking. And her career may not be over yet.

Audrey Hepburn: *One Wild Oat* 51, *Young Wives' Tale* 51, *Laughter in Paradise* 51, *The Lavender Hill Mob* 51, *Monte Carlo Baby* 52, *The Secret People* 52, *Roman Holiday* 53, *Sabrina* 54, *War and Peace* 56, *Funny Face* 57, *Love in the Afternoon* 57, *The Nun's Story* 59, *Green Mansions* 59, *The Unforgiven* 60, *Breakfast at Tiffany's* 61, *The Children's Hour* 62, *Charade* 63, *Paris When it Sizzles* 64, *My Fair Lady* 64, *How to Steal a Million* 66, *Two for the Road* 67, *Wait Until Dark* 67, *Robin and Marion* 76, *Bloodline* 77, *They All Laughed* 81.

The regal beauty of Katharine Hepburn has made her a screen goddess for more than 50 years.

Katharine Hepburn

Her beauty is in her bones, which is one reason why she alone among movie goddesses lost nothing by growing older. Her style is distinct and idiosyncratic. So is she. Katharine Hepburn is a woman of strong opinions, great self-confidence and imperious manner who leads her life as she sees fit and guards her privacy jealously. In her early years she did not sign autographs and she rarely grants interviews with the press today. In this she is reminiscent of Garbo. In another way she is like Garbo, too. She played the game by her own rules, not Hollywood's, and beat Tinseltown cold. Today the public adores her, the press worships her. Katharine Hepburn is America's answer to Garbo, Dietrich and the other great European-born legends of cinema.

Hepburn was born in 1909 in Hartford, Connecticut, into a family with many advantages. Her father was a successful doctor, an intellectual who admired George Bernard Shaw. Her mother, a suffragette and supporter of Margaret Sanger's birth control movement, had been educated in the finest Eastern schools and remained keenly interested in social issues all her life. There was discipline in the Hepburn home but freedom as well. Hepburn herself attended Bryn Mawr. Perhaps it is this background of New England, wealth and culture which makes Hepburn so brilliantly convincing when she plays a strict but compassionate schoolmarm or a no-nonsense lovable spinster. She was one of the few stars who preferred good roles to glamor.

Although Hepburn had her moments of meteoric rise she had her struggles, too. She started acting when she was 12, but as an amateur. She continued to perform in college and though she was ambitious, determined and competitive, her individualistic style was not accepted quickly by critics or theater-going audiences when she turned pro. In this age of Hepburn worship it's hard to believe how often critics panned her and how difficult it was for her even after she became a Hollywood star. From 1940 on she rarely attained top billing. She was voted box office poison in the late 1930s. Fan magazines criticized her for being temperamental, uncooperative and ungracious to her public. She was never one to suffer fools gladly.

Hepburn made her stage debut in Baltimore in 1928 in *The Czarina*, and went on to appear in *Death Takes A Holiday* and *Art and Mrs Bottle*. Nobody saw the star quality and she was often fired. Married in 1928 to Ludlow Ogden Smith, she was divorced in 1934. Along the way Hepburn was picked to play the lead in a modern version of *Lysistrata*, called *The Warrior's Husband*, which was produced in New York in 1932. Then she was dropped. So far, this is not a success story.

But time was on Hepburn's side. She was no quitter and when invited to rejoin *The Warrior's Husband*, she accepted. The play was a hit and bang, Hepburn became a Broadway star. Hepburn had already had some vague queries from Hollywood but nothing to lure her away from New York. Now she was in a strong position, and when RKO offered what seemed like a very sweet deal, she accepted. Then, par for the course in Hepburn's career, RKO began to waffle. Fortunately, George Cukor, who was about to do *A Bill of Divorcement* in 1932, was smarter than the studio brass and he insisted she play the part of John Barrymore's daughter. RKO signed her for five years.

The picture came out and, lo, a star appeared in the west. Rarely had a personality had the impact of Hepburn. Interestingly, critics tended to see her talent but not her beauty, though there was some recognition that she was a refreshing change from the vapid blondes that littered the Hollywood landscape. Lean, intelligent and sophisticated, it's hard to believe critics could be so blind to her good looks. But stereotypes were the admired norm in Hollywood.

Quickly, she won a best actress Academy Award for her role in *Morning Glory*, 1933. *Little Women*, too, 1933, was a perfect vehicle for her. She was wonderful as the forthright unflirtatious Jo, and George Cukor, who directed the film, considered it one of the best he'd ever made. The movie was a sensational hit and the reviews were raves.

But what followed next would have vanquished a lesser actress. Though Hepburn continued making films she decided to do a play in New York. She appeared in *The Lake*, which included the unfortunate line, 'The calla lilies are in bloom again'; comedians were to use it to poke fun at her for years. The critics also sharpened their knives. Describing Hepburn's performance, Dorothy Parker observed, 'She ran the gamut of emotions from A to B.' The show bombed.

Hepburn had no intention of proving little more than a ninety day's wonder, however, and she returned to Hollywood determined to recoup her ailing career. She fought for roles, defying the studio system rather than falling victim to it. But the movies that followed did little for her until once again she rode a rocket to the top with *Alice Adams*, 1935. It's a marvelous film which has held up beautifully over the years. Hepburn wanted George Stevens to direct the movie, and she wouldn't take no for an answer. Luckily, she won that studio battle. In the film Hepburn plays a sensitive girl, victimized by small-town snobbery and class distinctions. She deserved an Academy Award and was nominated but didn't get it. This wasn't the last time such a thing would happen to her.

Since *Little Women* Hollywood had liked Hepburn as a tomboy. In *Sylvia Scarlet*, 1935, she announces, 'Father, I'm going to cut my hair off! I'm going to be a boy!' Apparently Hollywood had a point, for she was much weaker in *Mary of Scotland*, 1936, than she was in *A Woman Rebels*, 1936, a costume drama dealing with the emancipation of women in Victorian times. Hepburn was never meant to be passive or simply pictorial. She

Above: Hepburn's fourth movie was *Little Women* (1933). From the left: Hepburn, Jean Parker, Joan Bennett, Frances Dee.

did best playing women with steel or fire at their core. She was memorable in *Stage Door*, 1937, but so far Hepburn had played serious or even tragic parts. Now she was about to enter a new phase of her career: screwball comedy.

Actually Hepburn was by nature the bold risk-taking type she played so well in comic films. Given flying lessons by Howard Hughes, she became quite a skilled aviator. In *Bringing Up Baby*, 1938, she did a different kind of flying, literally soaring as a comedienne in her role as society girl in charge of a leopard and in pursuit of Cary Grant. Neither she nor her co-star were upstaged by the big cat.

Typically, just as things were looking good for Hepburn they began to sour. She was sliding at the box office, which no matter what the reviews say, and hers were good at the time, is the absolute bottom line in Hollywood. RKO offered her a property she refused to do and she bought up her contract. It might have been the end for some actresses, but not Hepburn.

She had once understudied a play called *Holiday*. She knew it was an excellent vehicle for her and upon learning that Columbia had bought the screen rights, arranged to do it for them. She even got them to pay her more than RKO and to hire Cukor to direct. Down she may have been but out, never. *Holiday*, 1938, again linked Hepburn with Cary Grant, with the usual charming results. It's a Depression film. Hepburn is a rich young lady who receives a lesson in what real life is all about. Still, it was not the hit it should have been and there was little Hepburn could do but wait for something to turn up. Believe it or not, she was offered the part of Scarlett O'Hara in *Gone With The Wind*, but had the brains to keep her answer tentative. She was utterly wrong for the part and knew it, so when David O Selznick discovered Vivian Leigh and cast her instead, she took the loss calmly.

But there was no question that Hepburn needed a dazzler and one appeared, issuing from the pen of Philip Barry, who had written *Holiday*. It was *The Philadephia Story*. Hepburn played Tracy Lord, indulged and upper-class, who is about to embark upon a second marriage. The play is a light romantic comedy about the rivalry for her hand, and she took it to Broadway. It was a smash, and made up for *The Lake*. The calla lilies were forgotten or at least forgiven and Hepburn, who had bought the movie rights to the play, sold them, with herself thrown in, to MGM. Cary Grant and James Stewart helped strengthen the movie's attraction. *The Philadelphia Story*, 1940, was not only a hit, restoring Hepburn to Hollywood stardom, but also it has remained a classic. Hepburn won the New York Critics' Best Actress of the Year Award for it.

Still, Hepburn needed a contract and when MGM acted shy she wooed them with another property she'd bought, and suggested that she and Spencer Tracy play

Below: Hepburn and Cary Grant in *The Philadelphia Story* (1940). He was her ex-husband trying to win her back.

Above: Katharine Hepburn is the only actress to have won the Academy Award for best actress four times.

Above: As the Welsh schoolteacher in a made for television version of *The Corn Is Green*.

the leads. The studio accepted the deal and it was the start of a beautiful friendship, both off-screen and on. Tracy and Hepburn became one of Hollywood's greatest teams. In the ten films they made together the chemistry was perfect. He was steady and low-key; she was histrionic. His voice was soft; his accent indeterminate American. Her voice was quavery and singsong; her accent Eastern Seaboard. With them the battle of the sexes was lively and liberated in tone and they exchanged their verbal barbs with style and grace.

Woman of the Year, 1942, presented the pair as wedded journalists whose marriage was very rocky indeed. The movie won Hepburn her MGM contract. *State of the Union*, 1948, and *Adam's Rib*, 1949, were the best of the Tracy–Hepburn lot. In *Adam's Rib* they faced off as lawyers on opposite sides of a murder case with the audience wondering if Hepburn would win the case but lose her husband.

Hepburn made movies without Tracy during this period and she also did Shakespeare and Shaw on stage. In 1951 she was back in films, appearing in what many consider her finest role, the prim and proper old maid chugging along the river in Africa with a slovenly Humphrey Bogart in *The African Queen*, 1951. Both played their parts superbly, and he got an Oscar. She

didn't. It seems a pity. Though Hepburn has won a record number of Academy Awards, four in all, none in a supporting category, and also received more nominations than any other actress, her Oscars have never come when she deserved them the most.

The African Queen was an enormous success, putting the lie to the notion Hepburn was box office poison. Not only did the movie make a mint, it was generally rated one of the best pictures ever made. It still ranks high in over-all popularity. Hepburn had proved that a movie goddess need not fade as youth passes, or take on second-rate parts just to survive. The face that was so lovely in *Alice Adams* had changed, becoming a fine instrument for registering the emotions of a mature woman. The once sleek and elegant body was now wiry and expressive. Once again Hepburn had shown that she could triumph over conventional assumptions and remain a great star.

1952 saw *Pat and Mike*, another Tracy-Hepburn match-up. This one had her as an athlete and him as her trainer. It was her final MGM film. She was the archetypal spinster again when she appeared in *Summer Madness*, 1955. She did *The Rainmaker*, 1956, with Burt Lancaster. She was a stand-out in Tennessee Williams's bizarre *Suddenly Last Summer*, 1959, screenplay by Gore Vidal,

Above: Hepburn starred with Humphrey Bogart in *The African Queen* (1951), playing the daughter of a missionary.
Below: Hepburn played another preacher's daughter in *Rooster Cogburn* (1975), opposite John Wayne.

Below: The last film Henry Fonda made before his death was *On Golden Pond* (1981), co-starring with Hepburn. Each of them won an Academy Award for their work in this film about a very human elderly couple.

Above: One of the many successful films co-starring Hepburn and Spencer Tracy was *Woman of the Year* (1942).

Below: Hepburn and Cary Grant in *Bringing Up Baby* (1938). In the screwball comedy, 'Baby' was a baby leopard.

with Elizabeth Taylor and Montgomery Clift. Eugene O'Neill's masterpiece, *Long Day's Journey Into Night*, 1962, was a change of pace for Hepburn. A labor of love for the entire cast, which included Ralph Richardson, Jason Robards, and Dean Stockwell, the movie reveals Hepburn as the tormented drug-addicted mother in a tragic family, past hope, beyond salvation. She gave a moving twisted performance in her uniquely original style.

In 1967, *Guess Who's Coming to Dinner*, the last of the Tracy–Hepburn movies came out. It was the peak of the Civil Rights movement and the film, with Sidney Poitier, had a lot to say on the subject. The public loved the movie. It earned over 20 million dollars and got Hepburn another Oscar at last. It had been a long time since *Morning Glory*. There was a touch of sorrow to the movie. Spencer Tracy hadn't long to live. Her affection didn't waver and she was often at his bedside when he was dying.

The Lion in Winter, 1968, was a middle-brow historical costume drama, pitting Hepburn as a wily and astute but endearing Eleanor of Aquitaine against Peter O'Toole's aging vulnerable Henry II. They both turned in good but not stunning performances and Hepburn walked off with another Oscar.

Hepburn was fast on her way to becoming as big a legend as Eleanor of Aquitaine herself. She was on the top ten list of stars and seemingly in demand everywhere. She did a Broadway show, *Coco*, based on the famous French fashion designer, Coco Chanel. Other movies followed. On television, she played the aged Southern belle, Amanda, in *The Glass Menagerie*, 1973, Tennessee William's classic play. Again for television she appeared opposite the great Lawrence Olivier in *Love Among the Ruins*, 1975. *Rooster Cogburn*, 1975, was a movie which co-starred John Wayne, one of Hollywood's other extraordinary legends. She was a school teacher yet one more time in *The Corn Is Green*, 1978, on television, saving a Welch boy from a life in the mines. She was vibrant.

1981 was the year of Hepburn's next triumph, *On Golden Pond*, co-starring Henry Fonda. It was his last film, a wonderful sentimental vehicle for both. The film was a tribute to two illustrious careers and a farewell gesture by and for Fonda. Both stars received Academy Awards.

The struggles have receded, the ups and downs of Hepburn's career seem frail in comparison to her legend. But it is precisely because she had to work so hard, precisely because she had to swim against the Hollywood current that her success seems so phenomenal. Katharine Hepburn, actress and tenacious individualist, was no one's creation except her own. She made the world take note and accept her on her own terms. If our stars are a kind of royalty, then Katharine Hepburn wears the crown.

Above: With Montgomery Clift in *Suddenly Last Summer* (1959), based on a macabre one-act play by Tennessee Williams.

Above: Hepburn co-starred with Spencer Tracy in the last film he made— *Guess Who's Coming to Dinner* (1967).

Katharine Hepburn: *A Bill of Divorcement* 32, *Christopher Strong* 33, *Morning Glory* 33, *Little Women* 33, *Spitfire* 34, *Break of Hearts* 34, *The Little Minister* 34, *Alice Adams* 35, *Sylvia Scarlet* 35, *Mary of Scotland* 36, *A Woman Rebels* 36, *Quality Street* 37, *Stage Door* 37, *Bringing Up Baby* 38, *Holiday* 38, *The Philadelphia Story* 40, *Woman of the Year* 42, *Keeper of the Flame* 42, *Stage Door Canteen* 43, *Dragon Seed* 44, *Without Love* 45, *Undercurrent* 46, *Sea of Grass* 47, *Song of Love* 47, *State of the Union* 48, *Adam's Rib* 49, *The African Queen* 51, *Pat and Mike* 52, *Summer Madness* 55, *The Rainmaker* 56, *The Iron Petticoat* 56, *Desk Set* 57, *Suddenly Last Summer* 59, *Long Day's Journey Into Night* 62, *Guess Who's Coming to Dinner* 67, *The Lion in Winter* 68, *The Madwoman of Chaillot* 69, *The Trojan Women* 71, *A Delicate Balance* 73, *The Glass Menagerie* 73, *Rooster Cogburn* 75, *Love Among the Ruins* 75, *The Corn is Green* 78, *Olly, Olly Oxen Free* 78, *On Golden Pond* 81.

Grace Kelly—a true princess.

Grace Kelly

Alfred Hitchcock once described Grace Kelly as a woman with 'sexual elegance.' She was fire under ice. Coolly sophisticated, every inch a well-bred lady, she had but to smile to become a fresh and lovely colleen. Grace lived a rich full life. Born to wealth, she was an important movie star who became even more famous as Monaco's Princess Grace. In 1982 she died in a car accident and the world went into mourning along with Monaco. During her lifetime she'd come to symbolize good taste, restraint and high standards. In the 50s when most movie stars were blatant sex symbols, Grace Kelly was Hollywood's subtle blonde.

She was born in Philadelphia on 12 November 1929. Her family was wealthy, but definitely not members of the city's old-line elite. Grace's grandfather had come from Ireland. His children did very well for themselves in America and Grace's father owned a successful construction company. The Kellys were high achievers, especially when it came to sports. Grace's father won an Olympic medal in sculling and her brother would also be a champion in the same sport. Grace, the least athletic of the lot, liked swimming, horseback riding and tennis. Despite the family money, Grace was taught to sew and cook as a child as the Kellys placed a high value on self-reliance and independence.

Grace attended parochial and private schools and upon graduation from Stevens School shocked her family by saying she wanted to become an actress. Even though Grace's uncle George Kelly was a well-known playwright and the clan numbered at least one successful vaudevillian, Grace's parents had expected their daughter to choose a more conventional career. She went to New York, studying at the American Academy of Dramatic Arts. A hard worker, and highly disciplined, she started modeling in her free time. Soon she was earning four hundred dollars a week, posing for advertisements—hardly surprising, since she had a flawless complexion, a beautiful bone structure and was glitteringly photogenic.

Grace's true love was the stage. She adored New York and would have been content to stay there. She even turned down a movie contract while she was still a student. But she seemed destined for Hollywood. Appearances on television's *Philco Playhouse* and *Treasury Men in Action* brought her a bit part in a 1951 movie called *Fourteen Hours*. Again she was offered a film contract and again she refused.

But she couldn't resist the chance to play opposite Gary Cooper in *High Noon*, 1952, and accompanied by several members of her family she went to California. From the start there was much about Hollywood that disagreed with Grace. She was a very private person with serious goals. She had played the part of Raymond Massey's daughter in a Broadway production of Strindberg's *The Father* in 1949, and she didn't want to make bad movies or be just another 'Hollywood blonde.'

Then MGM came along with *Mogambo*, 1953, its

Above: Grace Kelly's first acting break was as the Quaker wife of Gary Cooper in *High Noon* (1952).
Below: With Ava Gardner in *Mogambo* (1953).

remake of *Red Dust*. Grace was asked to play the cool English woman whom Gable falls for. *Red Dust* was funnier but *Mogambo* was a good film. Grace was sufficiently aloof, then properly passionate, when she suddenly returns Gable's ardor. She was to win a Best Supporting Actress nomination for the role. But she still had qualms about MGM because she insisted that the studio permit her time off to do plays between films, before she'd sign a contract. Her wish was granted but her worries were not misplaced. Had it been left to MGM her movie career might have gone nowhere.

The studio had no idea what to do with Grace. Her composure, restraint and delicate beauty simply puzzled them. They wanted her to do cheesecake poses. She refused. They expected her to play a sleazy seductress. She said no. Then Alfred Hitchcock came to the rescue, borrowing Grace for *Dial M for Murder*, 1954. She was both stunning and exciting in the complicated tale of murder and villainy. He cast her again in *Rear Window*, 1954, one of his finest films. Grace was very Park Avenue in *Rear Window* but she let slip an occasional charged innuendo to co-star James Stewart which set the audience's imagination churning. Hitchcock believed that sex on film should be suspenseful, not blatant, and at last he'd found an actress who could provide plenty of precisely that kind of suspense.

MGM was pushing Grace hard to make a movie for them but she threatened to quit movies altogether and go back East if they didn't loan her out to Paramount for *The Country Girl*, 1954. She'd appeared briefly in Paramount's *The Bridges of Toko-Ri*, 1954, with William Holden. Knowing that she meant what she said, MGM agreed. Grace played a dowdy bitter woman in *The Country Girl*, doing her duty by staying with her alcoholic husband, Bing Crosby. Grace turned in an excellent performance and she won a Best Actress Academy Award, though most critics nowadays believe the Oscar should have gone to Judy Garland for *A Star Is Born*.

Grace had fought MGM hard and won but now she was trapped and she had to make *Green Fire*, 1954. It was a dud about emerald mines in South America; the studio even went so far as to use a cut-out of Grace's head on a bosomy body in a sexy green gown to advertise the film in front of New York's Broadway Theater. Grace had to pass the theater every day and it always made her lose her temper. When she turned down script after script, MGM placed her on suspension. But she said yes at last, only it was to Hitchcock.

She made what was to turn out to be a prophetic film, *To Catch A Thief*, 1955. It was a glamorous movie set in Monte Carlo and the French Riviera. The costumes and scenery were dazzling. Cary Grant was handsome and charming as usual. He plays a reformed cat burglar out to catch a thief impersonating his style. Grace pursues him, though with too much class for the word 'shamelessly' to apply. The movie is great fun as well as a superb mystery, though the car races along the twisting roads and hair-pin turns now leave one with an eerie shudder. It was on just such a road that Princess Grace would meet her death.

Two more pictures awaited Grace. First came *The Swan*, 1956, in which she appears as a beautiful princess, daughter of an impoverished noble family, who must marry a rich prince (Alec Guiness) when she really loves her suitor, Louis Jourdan. Again a movie script is reminiscent of her life. Its enough to make one super-stitious. *High Society*, 1956, was a delightful musical version of *The Philadelphia Story*. Bing Crosby and Frank Sinatra were in it. The movie was enormously popular everywhere but, of course, by now the world knew that Grace Kelly, movie star, was about to become Grace Kelly, royal personage.

Grace had met Prince Rainier at Monaco when she was in Europe for the Cannes Film Festival in 1955. Grace had kept her private life distinctly private though her name was linked with Oleg Cassini and Jean Pierre Aumont. Now she startled the press by announcing her engage-ment to His Serene Highness, Prince Rainier III, on 6 January 1956.

Monaco had gone into severe decline after its pre-war glory days as a playground for the very rich. Prince Rainier could not have chosen a better bride than Grace Kelly to help him restore the principality to its former brilliance. Under their guidance tourism increased and Monaco became a solvent little Mediterranean jewel.

There was a fabulous royal wedding in April 1956. Grace's trousseau was magnificent. She paid for it herself out of her movie salary and all the clothes were American-made, which helped endear her all the more to her home-based public.

Grace proved a truly worthy princess. She served as one of Europe's most gracious hostesses, devoted time and energy to charitable causes and was a caring mother to her three children: Princess Caroline, Prince Albert (heir to the throne) and Princess Stephanie.

There were always rumors that she would return to films. Hitchcock wanted her for *Marnie*. But something always seemed to get in the way and it was not to be. She did, however, present poetry readings under special circumstances. She was driving down to the Palace in Monaco with her daughter Stephanie from her informal home, Roc Agel, when her car went out of control (Grace may have had a slight stroke) and fell over a precipice. Stephanie was injured but Grace was an-nounced brain dead when she reached the hospital and it was a family decision to let her die. There was no hope. Her funeral was held 18 September 1982 and she was buried in the royal vault. Some of the light seemed to go out of Monaco with her.

Elusive, but never distant; demure, but never stuffy; Grace Kelly was legend, goddess, princess and star. She will be remembered forever as the American girl who succeeded in turning real life into fantasy.

Grace Kelly: *Fourteen Hours* 51, *High Noon* 52, *Mogambo* 53, *Dial M for Murder* 54, *Rear Window* 54, *The Country Girl* 54, *Green Fire* 54, *The Bridges at Toko-Ri* 54, *To Catch a Thief* 55, *The Swan* 56, *High Society* 56.

Kelly with William Holden in *The Country Girl* (1954). She won an Oscar as the wife of an alcoholic (Bing Crosby).

Bing Crosby sings 'True Love' to Kelly in *High Society* (1956). It was a musical version of *The Philadelphia Story*.

Hedy Lamarr's name became a household word meaning glamour.

Hedy Lamarr

Once upon a time in the land of make-believe (otherwise known as Hollywood) there was a beautiful actress named Barbara La Marr who died young. It was many years later during the era of talking pictures that Louis B Mayer of MGM finally found a woman beautiful enough to be worthy of the name Lamarr. She had hair as black as ebony, skin as white as snow, and thanks to cosmetics, lips as red as blood. In addition to beauty, she had wit, charm and style and led an adventurous life. Louis B Mayer predicted she would become a very great star, and she did.

Hedy (pronounced like lady) Lamarr was born in Vienna in 1913. Her real name was Hedwig Eva Maria Kiesler. At birth the good fairies sprinkled blessings upon her. Her father was a wealthy bank director. Her mother was a concert pianist who abandoned her career to care for her only child. Little Hedy lived in a big house, traveled to Paris, to Switzerland, to Ireland. She had private tutors, ballet lessons, piano lessons. She was sent to the finest of private schools and later to a finishing school.

In 1929 she managed to break into Austrian films and persuaded her parents to let her go to Berlin to study at Max Reinhardt's famous theater school. She did a couple of plays, more film work, and then came the movie which would bring her notoriety for years to come, *Symphonie er Liebe/Extase*, or as it was called in English, *Ecstasy*, 1933. In this day and age of full frontal nudity *Ecstasy* does not seem particularly scandalous, and in Europe the film won some awards for artistic merit. The picture tells the story of an impotent old man married to a beautiful young girl. The girl is shown swimming in the nude and running through the woods naked. There is a scene between the girl and a young man which some considered shocking, though all that was revealed was Hedy's face during passionate lovemaking.

However, shortly after the movie was made, Hedy married one of Europe's richest men, Austrian munitions maker Fritz Mandl. As Madame Mandl, Hedy had a position to maintain and her husband tried desperately to buy up all the copies of *Ecstasy* and destroy the film. He failed. Although thanks to her husband Hedy had servants, a fleet of cars, an enormous apartment in Vienna and a palace to call her own, in 1937 she went to Paris and got a divorce.

Hedy wangled a meeting with Louis B Mayer, who was in Europe looking for talent at the time, but Hollywood was in the grip of the Hays office and Mayer was worried about the impact of *Ecstasy*. But Hedy was never ordinary and predictable. She took the liner *Normandie* to New York on the same voyage as Mayer and by the time they reached America he was thoroughly captivated by her. Her gave her a contract and Hedy went to Hollywood, glad to escape the war clouds so ominously on the horizon in Europe and eager once more to have a career of her own.

Lamarr in *Lady of the Tropics* (1939), the story of the torrid romance between a half-native girl and a millionaire.

Lamarr starred with Charles Boyer in *Algiers* (1938), her first American film.

Although Hedy's exquisite appearance opened doors for her, she had to fight for roles in Hollywood like every other ambitious actress. It is a tribute to her that she was able to overcome not only the reputation she'd acquired from doing *Ecstasy* but also certain other obstacles. With her looks she would have reigned supreme had she arrived in Hollywood during the silent era or at the beginning of the decade. Mayer even compared her to Garbo. But times had changed.

America had grown bored with exotic European stars. Coy, cute and cuddly, the American girl was coming into her own on the motion picture screen. In something of a quandary over what to do with her, MGM loaned Hedy Lamarr out to Walter Wanger who was making a movie with Charles Boyer called *Algiers*, 1938. Hedy played a fascinating and romantic woman and Boyer murmured the famous line, 'Come with me to the Casbah' in her ear. Hedy became an overnight sensation. She even started the turban hat craze for women when she introduced the style in the film.

So far Hedy's life is the stuff of fairy tales but reality intervened. *Take This Woman* was supposed to be a dazzling Josef von Sternberg vehicle created just for her, but he was fired, the movie went through a lot of changes and revisions and was released late, 1940. It was no *Algiers*. *Lady of the Topics*, 1939, revealed Hedy as a beautifully costumed half-caste, but to maintain her stardom she needed a bigger and better film.

While waiting, Hedy continued her favorite hobby, painting. She also bought paintings, ultimately owning a valuable art collection. She went to parties and previews. On 4 March 1939 she met Gene Markey, a successful Hollywood producer and writer. She drove down to Mexico with him next day, and they made the impulsive decision to get married immediately. Back in California, Hedy and Gene adopted a son, but the marriage didn't last long.

Hedy got lucky again with *Boom Town*, 1940. It was the smash hit she'd needed. The public liked her with Gable so much in *Comrade X*, 1940, she was back with Gable again. This time she was a streetcar driver in Moscow and he was an American journalist. Directed by King Vidor, the picture was somewhat reminiscent of Garbo's *Ninotchka*, made the previous year, and it was extremely popular.

Hedy spent money with the same verve she made money and she knew better than to trust the studio to look after her interests. She battled the MGM bosses royally, over money, over contracts, over roles. They considered her temperamental and hard to get along with. As she saw it she was merely looking after herself. When it came to choosing scripts, though she sometimes made serious mistakes, turning down *Laura*, *Gaslight*, *Saratoga Trunk*, all big winners. She erred most when she rejected *Casablanca*. Who knows what it would have done for her career?

Above: Lamarr with Spencer Tracy in *I Take This Woman* (1940)—a dedicated doctor sacrifices all for Lamarr.

Below: Lamarr as the beautiful native girl in *White Cargo* (1942). Her most famous line was 'I am Tondelayo.'

Hedy mace a comedy with James Stewart, *Come Live With Me*, 1941 and a musical, *Ziegfeld Girl*, 1941, which included other MGM hot properties, like Lana Turner. *H M Pulham, Esq*, 1941, based on the John Marquand novel, won Hedy good reviews, and is one of her best films.

The Second World War was on and Hedy did her share at The Hollywood Canteen, greeting the GIs and signing autographs. There she met a fellow volunteer, English actor John Loder, who was making movies in Hollywood at the time. In 1943 he became husband number three and the father of Hedy's two children, daughter Denise and son Tony.

Hedy made more movies but *White Cargo*, 1942, stands out because this is the film where she played Tondelayo. Gone was the marble goddess Hedy, gone was the sophisticated Hedy. In her place was the sultry jungle passion flower Hedy. Her face and body covered with cocoa-butter, Hedy wore a sarong and made love to Walter Pidgeon in Pidgin English. GIs loved it.

The Heavenly Body, 1943, was a comedy co-starring William Powell. *Experiment Perilous*, 1944, Hedy's favorite movie, was a psychologically intriguing film with Paul Lukas as Hedy's fanatically jealous husband and George Brent as the doctor who saves her. She did the film on loan-out to RKO, then made *The Conspirators* for Warner Brothers in 1944. MGM made a bundle on the last film she did under contract to the studio, *Her Highness and the Bellboy*, 1945.

So famous was Hedy that she was now able to form her own production company. She seemed to belong to a special category of star, free to do pretty much as she pleased. Her European background, her cosmopolitan view of life off-screen, her grace and elegance on-screen kept her fans in awe. She acted like someone who deserved to be on a pedestal and the public gladly put her on one.

The Strange Woman, 1946, had Hedy playing a femme fatale. In 1947 she appeared with her ex-husband John Loder in *Dishonoured Lady*. 1950 was the year Hedy made *Samson and Delilah* for Cecil B De Mille and Paramount. A magnificent wardrobe of costumes was designed for Hedy, who had never made a movie in color before. Victor Mature was a muscular Samson, Hedy Lamarr was vividly beautiful as the Biblical temptress. The movie had the right blend of epic panorama, spicy sex and moralistic punishment to bring hordes of customers streaming into movie theaters. Hedy was happy and so was Paramount and director De Mille when the film turned out to be the number one box office success of the year.

Hedy followed up her success with Paramount by doing another picture for them, *Copper Canyon*, a technicolor Western, 1950, and she returned home to MGM for *A Lady Without Passport*, 1950. She had refused to do a personal appearance tour for Paramount,

Lamarr as the biblical beauty of *Samson and Delilah* (1950).

so when Bob Hope asked her to be his co-star in *My Favorite Spy* she was afraid Paramount would refuse to hire her. But they did and the 1951 movie was a good comedy.

By this time Hedy was well into her 30s and the movie business was changing radically. Hedy could still make $100,000 a picture, a decent sum now and a glorious sum then, but her days as a reigning Hollywood beauty were drawing to a close.

In Mexico she met Ted Stauffer, band leader turned Acapulco hotel owner, and married him. The marriage didn't work out and in less than a year she and her children were back in Beverly Hills. Hedy traveled. She bought scripts, even started a picture, but didn't complete it. In 1953 oil magnate W Howard Lee of Houston became her husband. Hedy moved to Texas with him and kept herself busy entertaining Houston's monied upper-crust. Howard built a resort lodge at Aspen, Colorado and named it in Hedy's honor. This marriage outlasted Hedy's previous excursions into matrimony but after six years, it, too, ended in divorce. It was not her last. In 1963, she married lawyer Louis J Boies.

Hedy's last three films were *The Face That Launched A Thousand Ships*, 1954, *The Story of Mankind*, 1957, and *The Female Animal*, 1957, in which she played an aging movie star who falls in love with the same man her daughter loves. In 1965 Hedy's fans were stunned when she was arrested for shop-lifting in a Wilshire Boulevard department store. She was found not guilty but despite several marriages to wealthy men and a career that spanned continents, Hedy was having real money problems.

Perhaps it was partly financial need that made Hedy turn to writing. In 1966 she published an autobiography called *Ecstasy and Me*, revealing many intimate details about herself and Hollywood. Unhappy with it, she later attempted to get an injunction against the book and sued her collaborators.

Independent in life, regal and remote on screen, Hedy Lamarr sets the standard of beauty for Hollywood goddesses. She is a study of balance, proportion and grace. Fashions may come and go, types and styles change, but no one will ever look at Hedy Lamarr on screen and ask, 'What did they ever see in her?'

Hedy Lamarr: *Ecstasy* 33, *Algiers* 38, *Lady of the Tropics* 39, *I Take This Woman* 40, *Boom Town* 40, *Comrade X* 40, *Come Live With Me* 41, *Ziegfeld Girl* 41, *H M Pulham Esq* 41, *Tortilla Flat* 42, *Crossroads* 42, *White Cargo* 42, *The Heavenly Body* 43, *The Conspirators* 44, *Experiment Perilous* 44, *Her Highness and the Bellboy* 45, *The Strange Woman* 46, *Dishonoured Lady* 47, *Let's Live a Little* 48, *Samson and Delilah* 50, *A Lady Without Passport* 50, *Copper Canyon* 50, *My Favorite Spy* 51, *The Face that Launched a Thousand Ships* 54, *The Story of Mankind* 57, *The Female Animal* 57.

The gorgeous Sophia Loren as she appeared in *Houseboat* (1959), in which she starred with Cary Grant.

Sophia Loren

She is an erotic dream. Yet she is famous for far more than her beauty. She had warmth and good sense, dignity and talent. Born in the slums, a victim of war, she rose to stardom in Italy and became an international celebrity. She has won a Best Actress Academy Award, an amazing achievement for a woman who is a sex symbol. It was an honor that would elude Marilyn Monroe. Her long relationship with husband Carlo Ponti is practically unique in the volatile world of film making. She is a devoted mother, a loyal daughter and an affectionate sister. She is a success story. She is Sophia Loren.

Sophia Scicolone was born in Rome in 1934, an illegitimate child. Her mother, a beautiful woman who once won a Greta Garbo look-alike contest, returned to her native village, Pozzuoli, near Naples, when Sophia was still a baby. It was a poor village and life was very hard. The stigma of illegitimacy made it that much harder. But Sophia had an extended family of grandparents, uncles and aunts, as well as a mother who loved her to soften her troubles. When Sophia was four, her mother had a second child, another girl. The children's father, who lived in Rome, either neglected them or showed active hostility toward them. When Sophia grew up, he re-entered her life, trying to get money out of her, even suing her for libel.

During the Second World War Sophia and all her neighbors suffered terribly. She went hungry, saw people shot in the streets, lived through bombing attacks. By the time the war ended Sophia was a survivor in the fullest sense of the word. She emerged into the light of the post-war world as a beautiful and voluptuous young girl who won a beauty contest at 14. Sophia's mother had once had ambitions of her own and she was eager to leave the confines of village life, so she took her two daughters to Rome and tried to get Sophia into the movies. It seemed a rash thing to do at the time but it was to pay off far beyond anyone's wildest dreams.

Sophia found work as an extra and appeared in 'fumettis,' popular magazines which told soap-opera-type stories through still photographs. She tried very hard to get better parts in films but met with a great deal of discouragement. Despite her great beauty her early screen tests were unpromising, and the competition in Rome was fierce. However, she had caught the eye of film producer Carlo Ponti, partner of Dino de Laurentiis. He tried to help her, though not in any spectacular way. She was still very young and their love affair was a few years down the road.

The initial impetus for Sophia's career may have come from her mother, but by this time the young girl herself had developed an iron determination to succeed as an actress. She worked hard, supporting both her mother and sister, and that left little time for youthful fun. No wonder she was shy, serious, and seemed older than her years. She'd taken the name Sofia Lazzaro but in 1952 changed it to Sophia Loren, which stuck. At last she got a break, *Aida*, 1953. She supplied the looks, Renata Tebaldi supplied the voice, and Ponti gave Sophia a contract.

Her roles improved and she was becoming known outside as well as inside Italy, but strictly as a sex object. When Vittorio de Sica cast her as a Neapolitan shopkeeper in *Gold of Naples*, 1955, she surprised her critics by turning in a very good performance. De Sica, a fellow Neapolitan, was a marvelous director for her, and she learned much of her craft from him. The movie went far to establish her as a serious actress within Italy. She began to appear with some of Italy's most gifted film actors, among them, Marcello Mastroianni. She and Mastroianni would work together many times, and each would attain the heights of stardom.

Sophia was becoming the darling of photographers and it was inevitable that she and Gina Lollobrigida would compete in a game of public rivalry. How real the whole thing was, who can say, but it got Italy's two leading beauties a lot of attention.

It was the international era of films but Hollywood was still a vital center and so Sophia made *Boy On A Dolphin*, 1957, co-starring Alan Ladd. She'd just finished *The Pride and the Passion*, 1957, playing Frank Sinatra's Spanish mistress who is attracted to Cary Grant. *The Pride and the Passion* turned out to be a momentous movie for her, not so much professionally as personally.

Sophia had been Carlo Ponti's mistress for some time now. He had a wife and two children in Italy and, though his wife was willing to grant him a divorce, he was having great difficulty obtaining one. As a public figure, Ponti had become the target of Catholic groups in Italy strongly opposed to divorce, and he and Sophia were held up as examples of a couple living in sin. Matters came to a head when Cary Grant fell in love with Sophia. He proposed marriage. But Ponti won out in the competition and engineered a rather complicated Mexican divorce and proxy marriage to Sophia.

Their troubles were not over, however. The public was urged to boycott their films and they were not permitted to return to Italy. The case dragged on for years with the Pontis slipping in and out of Italy as best they could, considering that the authorities could arrest Ponti at any time for bigamy. Moving to France, they married again, hoping to satisfy Italian legal requirements. Their situation was reminiscent of the furor created by Ingrid Bergman's affair with Roberto Rossellini years earlier.

Sophia made Eugene O'Neill's *Desire Under the Elms*, 1958, with Anthony Perkins and Burl Ives for Paramount. Next came *The Key*, 1958, in Britain, followed by *Houseboat*, 1958, with Cary Grant. Sophia and Cary Grant looked good together and the wedding they hadn't had in real life they got on the screen. *Black Orchid*, 1959, cast Sophia with Anthony Quinn and her

Above: Loren starred with Charlton Heston in *El Cid* (1961), about the man who drove the Moors from Spain.
Below: As her own mother in a TV autobiographical film.

Above: Sophia Loren, the sensuous Italian beauty.
Below: Loren starred with Marlon Brando in *A Countess from Hong Kong* (1967), which was directed by Charles Chaplin.

performance won her Best Actress at the Venice Film Festival. Despite the hue and cry against her in Italy she was greeted warmly by the Venetians when she arrived.

That Kind of Woman, 1959, had her playing opposite Tab Hunter but the chemistry wasn't right. She was the star of a troupe of strolling players in *Heller in Pink Tights*, 1960, with Anthony Quinn again. She was good with Clark Gable in *It Started in Naples*, 1960, and the movie was popular. *A Breath of Scandal/Olympia*, 1960, presented her as a Hapsburg princess who falls in love with American John Gavin.

Sophia's Hollywood era was over. She was far more comfortable in Europe. In 1961 came the movie of her dreams, *La Ciociara/Two Women*, a film about a woman and her young daughter trying to survive during the war, who are raped by a band of soldiers. It was an incredibly moving film, not at all an exploitation picture, and it allowed Sophia to draw on the resources of her own sufferings during the war. She won an Oscar, the first ever given to an actress in a foreign language film, and she won the Best Actress Award at the Cannes Film Festival, too, proving perhaps that Sophia works best in her own native Italy.

However, she went on to make *El Cid* in Spain, 1961, with Charlton Heston. The movie lacked fire. But she was delightful again in *Boccaccio '70*, 1962, the de Sica episode in a three-part film. *Madame Sans Gêne*, 1962, increased her European fame and for the second time in two years she was considered the best Foreign Actress in France's Cinémonde poll. These were prolific years for her and one of her favorite movies was *The Fall of the Roman Empire*, 1964. She played the daughter of Alec Guiness, an actor she admired enormously.

It was back to Italy where *Yesterday, Today and Tomorrow*, 1964, and *Marriage Italian Style*, 1964, both with Mastroianni, were two of her biggest international successes. In part, the movie's acclaim was due to Sophia's beauty. Never had she looked more sensual. At that moment there was no woman on screen who could rival Sophia's loveliness.

Operation Crossbow, 1965, had Sophia playing a Dutch war widow. In *Judith*, 1966, she was the Jewish wife of a war criminal, assisting the Israeli underground. *A Countess from Hong Kong*, 1967, was another important film for her because she felt honored to work with Charlie Chaplin. She got better reviews than the film itself.

In 1969 she won the Golden Globe, which is presented each year to the world's most popular star by the United States Press Association Foreign Corps. But the most important thing about 1969 for Sophia was the birth of a son. She had long wanted to have a child, but had suffered from a series of miscarriages. Sophia was heroic during her pregnancy, staying in bed for months, submitting to any treatment that would help her deliver a baby. She received many letters of congratulations from

Above: Loren won as Oscar for *Two Women* (1961).　　　　　　*Below:* She starred with David Niven in *Lady L* (1965).

Marilyn Monroe

Marilyn is more than a legend. She's a myth. Arthur Miller, one of America's leading playwrights, wrote a play about his marriage to her called *After The Fall*. Norman Mailer, one of America's leading authors, wrote a book about her called *Marilyn*. She's been the subject of television shows and even of a musical. Marilyn Monroe is Hollywood's most tragic beauty queen.

A sexy angel whose softness and vulnerability made her irresistible to men in those pre-women's lib days of the 1950s, Marilyn is mythic because she wasn't a survivor. She had a touch of what other stars have. Her comic talent for playing the dumb blonde is in a league with Harlow's. But she lacked Harlow's brittle sarcasm. Her sashaying walk was almost as great a parody of female sexuality as Mae West's. But she had none of Mae's toughness and confidence. Her blonde hair, baby voice and innocent face are more reminiscent of Shirley Temple than Marlene Dietrich. But the body that comes with the face is very grown-up.

All told Marilyn isn't really like anybody else. She's one of a kind, a vamp who was never calculating, a brazen hussy who never played the villain. Its not surprising Americans love her for they always root for the underdog and Marilyn had a knack for winding up the loser.

She was born Norma Jean Baker in Los Angeles in 1926. Her troubles started early, for her birth was illegitimate at a time when such things counted. Marilyn's childhood was spent in orphanages and foster homes, since her mother spent most of her life in mental hospitals. Lonely and insecure, Marilyn married in her early teens, but she'd been raped and abused as a child and the marriage was more an act of desperation than of love. It didn't last. During World War II Marilyn worked in a munitions factory, but she had her dreams. In 1946 she joined a prominent modeling agency and her pictures began to appear in magazines. But instant stardom didn't follow.

Marilyn was merely one of countless disadvantaged young girls trying to make it up out of poverty against the odds. Needing money badly, in the late 1940s she posed nude for a calendar, then a rather shocking thing to do. The calendar would return to haunt her on her way up in Hollywood but she was clever and managed to use the calendar to enhance her image as America's number one sex symbol. She was also quite witty about it, for Marilyn realized that spoofing sex got you a lot farther than taking it too seriously.

She was noticed in passing by Howard Hughes and that got her an agent and a screen test. She was marvelously photogenic. Marilyn was one of those stars who seems to coo to a camera. But, lacking money, special contacts or anything else that helps one get ahead in life, Marilyn was just another face in the crowd. She did land a contract with 20th Century Fox which paid her a pittance, but she was edited out of her first film and had

Monroe appeared in the gaudy musical *There's No Business Like Show Business* (1954). She is on the right.

a bit part in a third-rater about juvenile delinquents called *Dangerous Years*, 1947.

At least it was a start and it enabled Marilyn to use what she had, namely her beauty, to get ahead. She began making lots of friends, chiefly male. But this hardly made her unique in Hollywood and the help she received was minimal. Ironically, of all the film goddesses, self-destructive and dependent Marilyn comes closest to creating her career herself. No stage mother pushed her; no producer discovered her; there were no rich relatives to send her checks.

She was signed by Columbia after 20th Century dropped her. She and Adele Jergens were leads in *Ladies of the Chorus*, 1948, and Marilyn was described as 'promising' by the *Motion Picture Herald*, but the studio dropped her anyway. She continued doing bit parts as best she could until she got a new agent, Johnny Hyde. He recognized her talent and got her the part of Louis Calhern's mistress in *The Asphalt Jungle*, 1950, a good thriller. Though the part wasn't much, Marilyn was. The audience took to her. She was gorgeous again in *All About Eve*, 1950, playing, as usual, the kind of girl you love and leave.

Still there was no magic for Marilyn and hard times followed. She appeared in a few more movies. Then her agent got her a deal at 20th Century Fox, but it was nothing special. She hung around and was at last given a contract which started her at 500 dollars a week, to reach

1500 a week after seven years—an improvement, but not the stuff of stardom. She was to be the studio's standard 'little broad,' to be used whenever such a part was required.

Still dreaming, Marilyn held on, right through *As Young As You Feel*, 1951, *Love Nest*, 1951, and *Let's Make It Legal*, 1951. But if the studio bigwigs couldn't see her for dust, the public recognized a potential star. The engaging but fluffy-headed little blonde from whom sex appeal simply flowed was winning a big following. Marilyn was a born scene stealer.

The 20th Century Fox publicity department mailed out her pictures and the media took note. Marilyn began to get a lot of attention from the press. *Clash by Night*, 1951, was an RKO movie but it may have helped wake 20th Century's studio head, Darryl Zanuck, up. His famous blonde star of the 1940s, Betty Grable, was growing older. He needed a new blonde and Marilyn was it.

Several lackluster films followed until she appeared as a stenographer in *Monkey Business*, 1952, with Cary Grant. She was adorable. Her salary was climbing fast when she did *Niagara* in 1953. This was her first breakaway film. She was lusciously sexy and the fans howled for more.

Gentlemen Prefer Blondes, 1953, was next on 20th Century's star-building agenda. An adaptation of the Broadway musical, it had Marilyn sparkle her way through the role of Lorelei Lee who believes firmly that

Above : Clark Gable nuzzles Monroe in a scene from *The Misfits* (1961) — the last film either of them made.
Below : The famous Monroe nude calendar photo.

Above : Marilyn and Jane Russell in *Gentlemen Prefer Blondes* (1953), a story of husband-hunting.
Below : The most famous scene in *The Seven Year Itch* (1955).

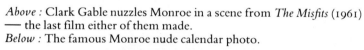

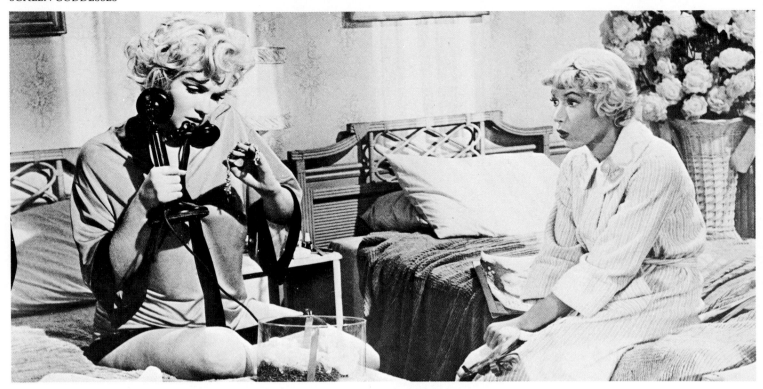

In *Ladies of the Chorus* (1948), Marilyn Monroe played the part of a chorus girl in a seedy burlesque house.

diamonds are a girl's best friend. *How To Marry A Millionaire*, 1953, was another gold digger's tale. It was also the second movie done in Cinemascope. Marilyn had no trouble filling the screen with her comic vitality. Her movies were now among Hollywood's top money-makers, and she as the number one female draw in the country. The little girl who had wanted to get inside the candy store had arrived but good.

To the public the Marilyn of this time was a sweet dopey kid, a bit of a joke, maybe, and not very talented, whom you'd sure like to bring home but not to meet mother. She was a singer of sorts, a dancer of sorts, a girl on a light-hearted romp. Although the facts of her unhappy childhood were known, the image of her as a woman victimized by men and destroyed by Hollywood would come later. When she married baseball's legendary hero, Joe DiMaggio, it was as if Marilyn had stepped out of one of 20th Century's spectacular musicals of the decade before. She was an American success story, the stuff of happy endings.

Marilyn entertained the boys in Korea and was rapturously received. She made Otto Preminger's *River of No Return*, 1954, essentially a cowboy film, and *There's No Business Like Show Business*, 1954, a musical with a star-studded cast. Marilyn's on-set problems began to surface in 1952. Eager to be accepted as a real actress, she took lessons, sought help from coaches and asserted herself with the studio. But her deep insecurities made it hard for her to fight effectively. Although she did force the studio to give her better material and she was to win her battle to make the kind of salary she deserved, the fight took a lot out of her. She was, despite her accomplishments, essentially fragile.

The Seven Year Itch, 1955, was a good vehicle for her.

She played a playful tempting little sexpot who had very-married Tom Ewell drooling and the movie was a hit. After this, Marilyn, who was getting the reputation of being 'difficult,' had another falling out with 20th Century Fox and escaped to New York where she studied at the Actors' Studio. Its director, Less Strasberg, considered her sensitive and talented.

Extravagant and now deeply in debt, Marilyn went back to Hollywood. Despite her frequent late arrivals on set, her many suspensions, her problems with directors and co-stars, 20th Century kept her on its roster. The reason is simple. She was by now the most valuable property in movies.

Bus Stop, 1956, revealed just how good Marilyn was when given the right role. The film is based on the William Inge play and co-stars Don Murray. Marilyn is touching and sad, as well as funny and sexy, as a singer who is wooed and won by a cowboy. The critics and the public loved the film but she was not nominated for an Academy Award. She still wasn't quite respectable.

Marriage to Arthur Miller in 1956 boosted Marilyn's stock with the intellectual community after the initial puzzlement died down. But the marriage wasn't really surprising. Marilyn may have acted dumb but she wasn't and she was certainly a charismatic personality. Next she did *The Prince and the Showgirl*, 1957, with Laurence Olivier. He directed the film but it was her production. She had artistic control and owned the rights to 75 percent of the profits. She was awsomely beautiful in the movie but she and Olivier did not get along and the picture isn't quite bubbly enough. Marilyn was now fighting regularly with most of her directors and co-stars. She was growing more unreliable by the day, not turning up at all sometimes, which sent film costs zooming. But though she was starting to crack, fine work still lay ahead.

Marilyn returned to California, sensibly turning down the chance to play Lola-Lola in a remake of *The Blue Angel*. That was definitely Dietrich's part. At the very least a remake by Marilyn would have been resented. Besides there was no way anyone, not even Marilyn, could improve on the original. She made *Some Like It Hot*, 1959, instead—a gem—with Tony Curtis and Jack Lemmon. She was irresistible as a singler with an all-girl orchestra, pursued by the relentless Curtis and Lemmon, who occasionally did their chasing in drag. By now Marilyn had her sad little bad little girl character down pat, and the movie was her biggest money-maker ever.

Marilyn made *Let's Make Love*, 1960, with Yves Montand, but it was extremely hard for her to hold herself together. She was relying more and more on sleeping pills and barbituates to see her through. In *The Misfits*, 1961, her last film, she looked thin and her face was drawn. Her marriage to Miller was dissolving and all she could look back on was a long chain of desperately inadequate relationships.

Her co-star in *The Misfits* was Clark Gable. It was to be his last movie, too. The film, with its background of capturing wild horses, was written by Arthur Miller, and it tells the moving story of two lost lonely people who find each other. Marilyn's performance is mature. Some fans found the movie too serious but it was one of Marilyn's best films.

By August of 1962 she was dead from an overdose of barbituates. The story that now unfolded about her last years was grim. She'd been in and out of psychiatric clinics, was drinking heavily, and was depressed about growing older. Out of the public shock and sorrow grew the legend.

Marilyn Monroe is the symbol of every sensitive girl Hollywood ever destroyed. She stands for all the abandoned children who dreamed of finding love and security someday and who found hopelessness and disillusionment instead. But she's more than a symbol of despair; she's also the image of beauty. In her films and in the many wonderful photographs she left behind she is simply the most beautiful girl in the world.

Marilyn Monroe: *Dangerous Years* 47, *Ladies of the Chorus* 48, *Love Happy* 49, *A Ticket to Tomahawk* 50, *The Asphalt Jungle* 50, *All About Eve* 50, *The Fireball* 50, *Right Cross* 50, *Home Town Story* 51, *As Young As You Feel* 51, *Love Nest* 51, *Let's Make It Legal* 51, *We're Not Married* 52, *Clash by Night* 51, *Full House* 52, *Monkey Business* 52, *Don't Bother to Knock* 52, *Niagara* 53, *Gentlemen Prefer Blondes* 53, *How to Marry a Millionaire* 53, *River of No Return* 54, *There's No Business Like Show Business* 54, *The Seven Year Itch* 55, *Bus Stop* 56, *The Prince and the Showgirl* 57, *Some Like It Hot* 59, *Let's Make Love, 60, *The Misfits* 61.

Above: Monroe in *The Prince and the Showgirl* (1957).
Below: A shot on the set of *The Misfits* (1961). Clift, Monroe, Gable, Wallach, John Huston, Arthur Miller.

Kim Novak, one of Hollywood's most beautiful stars.

Kim Novak

In the 50s Hollywood had a trio of famous blondes. One symbolized bouncy sex and innocent vulnerability. Her name was Marilyn Monroe. At the other end of the spectrum there was a cool elegant lady who represented sophistication and subtle sexuality. Her name was Grace Kelly. In the middle stood Kim Novak. She had a voluptuous figure, a whispery voice, and a beautiful sensitive face which made her a lot like Marilyn. But she also had a lady-like aura and a restrained classiness that made her a little like Grace Kelly. Of course, she was much more than a merger of the two. She had a haunting loveliness and a dreamy quality all her own which made her the perfect focus for the public's fantasies.

Kim's is a Cinderella story. In 1955 nobody had ever heard of her. A year later only Monroe topped her as a star. Her early background is prosaic. She was born in Chicago in 1933 where her father worked on the rail-road. She grew up wanting to be a movie star, and so went to Los Angeles hoping for a break. All she seemed to have going for her was beauty, and in Hollywood that's a common commodity like something you buy at the dime store, which by the way, is one of the places Kim Novak worked. She also ran an elevator and demon-strated refrigerators.

She did a walk-on in an RKO film called *The French Line*, 1954, and was spotted by Columbia's casting director. The studio system which had been strong and tight in the 1940s was in big trouble. Columbia Pictures had never been one of the super-sized studios like MGM, but it had produced one of the all-time great film goddesses, Rita Hayworth. Now Harry Cohn, the feisty head of Columbia, was on the look-out for a younger woman to follow in Rita Hayworth's footsteps. Nothing much went on at Columbia that he didn't know about and when Kim Novak came to his attention he picked her out as a girl with star quality.

Kim was under contract and earning 75 dollars a week when she was given a major part in *Pushover*, 1954, with Fred MacMurray. Kim proved photogenic and she had an air of glamor and mystery, so Harry Cohn decided to give his discovery the big push. Columbia was doing a comedy with Judy Holliday called *Phfft!*, 1954. They needed a blonde sex symbol to play the 'other woman' and they were on the verge of borrowing a star from another studio when Cohn chose Kim Novak for the part. Audiences loved Kim and she was given the night-club singer's role in *Five Against the House*, 1955, a thriller. Again, Kim won high ratings with the public.

At this point Cohn presented her with a diamond in the form of a really juicy role. William Inge's play, *Picnic*, was to be made into a movie which would star William Holden and Joshua Logan would direct. Kim would play the small-town beauty who succumbs to Holden. She sizzled on screen, exuding sex even as she came down a staircase or danced with Holden to the song *Moonglow*. It was *Picnic*, 1955, a smash hit in part because of her presence, that made Kim Novak a big star.

Kim was making a mere hundred dollars a week when Otto Preminger borrowed her from Columbia for 100

Above: Novak starred with William Holden in *Picnic* (1955). She was a small-town girl and he was a drifter.
Below: She starred with Sinatra and Hayworth in *Pal Joey* (1957).

thousand dollars to appear opposite Frank Sinatra in the film version of the Nelson Algren novel about a drug addict, *The Man With the Golden Arm,* 1955. The movie was enormously popular.

Kim's glamor appealed to women as well as men, which made her a star with truly mass appeal. In *The Eddy Duchin Story,* 1956, she played Tyrone Power's first wife and was ethereally lovely. The picture was one of the top ten money makers of the year. *Jeanne Eagles,* 1957, followed, a movie about the 1920s actress who took drugs and drank herself to death. Poor Kim was earning only 1000 dollars a week at the time so she got a mere 13 thousand dollars for *Jeanne Eagles* while her co-star Jeff Chandler got 200 thousand. But he'd been borrowed from another studio. In money terms, Kim was a victim of the studio system just as Ingrid Bergman and many other stars before her had been, making fortunes for others, not themselves. In 1956 *Box Office Magazine* conducted a poll and Kim was named the most popular star in America. Her agent concluded that she deserved 300 thousand dollars a film but Columbia was loath to give her any kind of raise.

This was Kim's peak moment in Hollywood but she lacked the leverage to bring Columbia to heel. The studio considered her its creation and product, and the critics by and large agreed. She lacked credibility as an actress and ultimately that was to hurt. She couldn't fight back by heading for Broadway or demanding parts with more scope and versatility. Academy Awards would not come her way. She was never able to establish herself as a perennial eccentric, idiosyncratic character or dominating force. Off-screen there were no wild scandals to keep her in the limelight. Though she was profiled by *Time Magazine* and photographs of her were everywhere, she was viewed strictly as a beauty, not a talent.

And beautiful indeed she was in *Pal Joey,* 1957, with Frank Sinatra and Rita Harworth. The movie was a hit though the critics panned it. Kim inherited Rita Hayworth's dressing room, definitely a prestigious gesture on Columbia's part. Alfred Hitchcock cast her in *Vertigo,* 1958, co-starring James Stewart. It's one of the master director's most famous suspense films. She made *Bell, Book and Candle,* 1958, again with Stewart. It's a charming movie about a sophisticated world of witches. The color photography is splendid and Kim is breathtaking. Throw in Jack Lemmon, Elsa Lanchester, Hermione Gingold, and the late Ernie Kovacs and you have what may be the best picture Kim ever made.

The Middle of the Night, 1959, *Strangers When We Meet,* 1960, and *Boys' Night Out,* 1962, followed. Kim was fighting hard for good material and getting the reputation of being temperamental. Columbia tried her in a comedy, *The Notorious Landlady,* 1962, with Jack Lemmon. But Kim and Columbia couldn't reach an understanding and she left the studio. In 1964 she appeared in a remake of the movie, *Of Human Bondage,* co-starring Laurence Harvey. The critics panned her performance and the film was a failure. Billy Wilder's *Kiss Me Stupid*, 1964, offended many critics and exhibitors but it has its defenders and Kim as a waitress hired for a one-night stand turns in one of her finest performances. *The Amorous Adventures of Moll Flanders*, 1965, was a romp. She married her co-star, Richard Johnson. They were divorced a year later.

Not until 1968 was she on screen again. She made *The Legend of Lylah Clare*. Kim's role was based on the personalities of several movie goddesses, a neat piece of casting. Warner's put her in a comedy, *The Great Bank Robbery*, 1969, with theater genius Zero Mostel.

Kim did a television movie called *The Third Girl From the Left*, 1974, with Tony Curtis, and once again followed Rita Hayworth's footsteps, taking over her part in *Tales That Witness Madness*, 1973, when Rita pulled out of the picture. After all her years of being underpaid by Columbia, Kim received 100 thousand dollars for the role. She made *Satan's Triangle* in 1975. She was well-paid again earning 50 thousand dollars for three days work in *The White Buffalo*, 1977, which starred Charles Bronson, and she did a German film, *Gigolo Armer Gigolo/Just a Gigolo*, 1978, with rock star David Bowie. In *The Mirror Cracked*, 1980, with rival film goddess Elizabeth Taylor, Kim was delightful. Not only was she funny in this film version of Agatha Christie's mystery novel, she still looked gorgeous. She'd showed her sense of humor in another way, too, five years earlier. An ardent animal lover, she solved a lot of medical expenses in one fell swoop, by marrying her veterinerian.

Kim Novak was the last movie goddess to emerge from the Hollywood studio system. Had she appeared on the scene a decade or two earlier her career might have been even better, since she would have been perfect in technicolor historical epics where the heroine sweeps across the screen in one beautiful costume after another. She was meant, too, for light romantic comedy in sophisticated settings and such material was hard to come by in her era.

As it is, she has left a stunning visual imprint on film. Sexy and yet mysterious, she is the portrait of a movie goddess, a blonde and beautiful ideal for her fans to love.

Kim Novak: *The French Line* 54, *Pushover* 54, *Phfft!* 54, *Five Against the House* 55, *Son of Sinbad* 55, *Picnic* 55, *The Man With the Golden Arm* 55, *The Eddie Duchin Story* 56, *Jeanne Eagles* 57, *Pal Joey* 57, *Vertigo* 58, *Bell, Book and Candle* 58, *Middle of the Night* 59, *Strangers When We Meet* 60, *Pépé* 60, *Boys' Night Out* 62, *The Notorious Landlady* 62, *Of Human Bondage* 64, *Kiss Me Stupid* 64, *The Amorous Adventures of Moll Flanders* 65, *The Legend of Lylah Clare* 68, *The Great Bank Robbery* 69, *Tales That Witness Madness* 73, *Third Girl From the Left* 73, *Satan's Triangle* 75, *The White Buffalo* 77, *Just a Gigolo* 78, *The Mirror Cracked* 80.

Above: Novak in the costume piece, *The Amorous Adventures of Moll Flanders* (1965).
Below: She played the stage star *Jeanne Eagles* (1957) with Jeff Chandler.

Elizabeth Taylor, a spectacular beauty, who has probably had more press coverage than any other star.

Elizabeth Taylor

Say 'movie star' and you think of Elizabeth Taylor. Beautiful beyond belief, she has fascinated the public since she was a child star and is perhaps the most famous woman in the world; certainly she is one of the richest. Her life is as exciting and romantic as a fable out of *The Arabian Nights*. She has been at the swirling center of scandals which won her headlines and if we count Richard Burton twice she's been married no less than seven times, with an eighth looming on the horizon. Professionally, her films have grossed a fortune; she's won two Academy Awards, and, recently, has become a success on Broadway. If more drama is required, Liz (she's one of the few stars whose nickname is used casually by just about everybody) has been at death's door several times because of serious bouts of illness. What's more, unlike some actresses who guard their privacy or were protected from the press by the studios, Elizabeth's entire life has always been on view. She is a public phenomenon.

Elizabeth Taylor was born in London in 1932. Her parents were Americans who ran an art gallery in England but they returned to America at the start of World War II, moving to Los Angeles. Elizabeth's mother, Sara, had been an actress when she was young and since her small daughter was already a beauty she felt the child might have a future in films. Universal Studios put Elizabeth in *There's One Born Every Minute*, 1942. Today the picture's only claim to fame is that it was the vehicle for Elizabeth's debut.

Elizabeth really came to the fore when she made *Lassie Come Home*, 1943, with Roddy McDowall, who was to become a lifelong friend. She was under contract to MGM at the time, the ideal studio for her, since it had vast promotional resources. Liz, ever accompanied by the ambitious Sara, a true stage mother, lived the usual life of a child performer. She took myriad lessons in dancing, elocution and the rest, attended the MGM school and posed for publicity shots.

Elizabeth's screen presence was magical from the start. There was a fragility to her beauty when she was a child which the camera captured well and she was a promising actress. She turned in a touching performance as the consumptive little waif in *Jane Eyre*, 1944, but the movie which made her a first-class star was *National Velvet*, 1944, based on the Enid Bagnold novel. Elizabeth occupied a special position as Hollywood's favorite little English girl even before she won the coveted role of Velvet Brown. The MGM publicity department had played up her English background for sentimental reasons during the war.

Elizabeth was really wonderful in *National Velvet*, one of the best girl-loves-horse stories ever. An ardent animal lover then as now, she wrote a charming book called *Nibbles and Me* about her pet chipmunk, painted as a hobby, and presented the image of a rather elegant young lady at the turning point of adolescence. Had her career ended at that moment she would still have been more than a passing footnote in the history of films.

But Elizabeth's career didn't end. She was to perform a near miracle and make a successful transition from child to adult star. What's more she was to achieve the tran-

Even as a child, Taylor was a great beauty. She was only 11 when she made *Lassie Come Home* (1943).

Mickey Rooney gives her a haircut so that she can pass for a jockey in *National Velvet* (1944).

sition without being destroyed in the process. Other young products of the studio star-making system might become alcoholics, drug addicts, suicidal or psychotic— not Elizabeth. Despite all her emotional ups and downs she was to prove a sane and tough survivor.

Elizabeth, with her raven-black hair, violet eyes and sensual figure, mature beyond its years, was growing up to be a sensation. MGM cast her in a series of teen-age movies to keep her before the public but they were really holding her in reserve for bigger things later and they kept the tone of her films low-key.

Gossip columnists Louella Parsons and Hedda Hopper no longer dwelt on Elizabeth's fondness for puppies and kittens. She had reached the age for boys. But Elizabeth was no Lolita. Fan magazines were filled with articles about how poor little Liz couldn't get a date. This seems improbable but it is true that during her teen years she had little opportunity to meet other adolescents, and when she did it was hardly under normal circumstances. It was the price she paid for being a valuable studio property.

In the movies she made during this phase of her career she generally played a rich, spoiled, but basically conventional and essentially sympathetic young girl. Ironically, it was a part she would often play in real life. *Cynthia*, 1947, was the first of the lot. *A Date With Judy*, 1948, is perhaps the most well-known. It was a step up for Elizabeth when she was cast as Amy in the remake of *Little Women*, 1949. She was ravishing.

Taylor starred with Montgomery Clift in *A Place in the Sun* (1951). The picture won six Academy Awards.

1950 was the year of Elizabeth's first marriage. She wed Nicky Hilton, heir to the fabulous Hilton Hotels fortune. The wedding itself was stunningly opulent and Elizabeth in a white gown was the image of the bride beautiful. MGM also chose to release her movie *Father of the Bride*, 1950, with Spencer Tracy, in time to cash in on the wedding publicity which was enormous. This, too, was to become a pattern in Elizabeth's life. She would often make films which capitalized on her private amours and vice versa.

Father's Little Dividend, 1951, was a sequel to *Father of the Bride*. But Elizabeth's marriage to Nicky Hilton was a failure and by 1951 she was divorced. Elizabeth's next big movie was *A Place in the Sun*, 1951, a fine film, based roughly on Theodore Dreiser's *An American Tragedy*. Elizabeth played the rich and beautiful girl every man dreams of marrying. Montgomery Clift was the tormented young man trapped by poverty.

Elizabeth was a lovely Rebecca in *Ivanhoe*, 1952. The press was out in full force again when she married English actor Michael Wilding. The couple had two children. She continued to make movies but it wasn't until 1956 that she got a really important part again. This was *Giant*, based on the Edna Ferber novel, co-starring the mythic James Dean. It was a big epic film which allowed Elizabeth to play a somewhat tougher woman than her usual role.

1957 saw her divorced from Michael Wilding. She made *Raintree County*, 1957, again with Montgomery Clift. By now he was both friend and mentor. She was to remain loyal to him through the rest of his short tragic life, even attempting to resurrect his career when no one else would hire him. *Raintree County* brought her an Oscar nomination for her role as a twisted Southern belle.

Elizabeth was now the wife of colorful impressario Mike Todd. Born in poverty, Todd made, lost, and remade fortunes. Their life together was splashy. Todd threw huge parties for her and gave her dazzling jewels. The couple traveled around the world promoting Todd's various schemes and productions and the media had a field day. A daughter, Liza, was born to Elizabeth in 1958 but Todd died in a plane crash not long after.

Almost instantly Elizabeth was back in the news over her love affair with singer and friend of Todd's, Eddie Fisher. Eddie was married to Debbie Reynolds at the time and public opinion generally sided with Debbie and against Elizabeth. Whatever she was really like, the media cast Debbie as a wholesome all-American girl-type, devoted mother, and the injured party. Elizabeth was the vamp who 'stole' Debbie's husband. The whole incident became an enormous scandal culminating in Elizabeth's marriage to Eddie. The scandal did not hurt Elizabeth's career and her salary climbed into the stratosphere.

Elizabeth's next big movie was *Cat on a Hot Tin Roof*, 1958, taken from the Tennessee Williams play. Paul Newman plays the hero who sexually rejects wife Maggie, memorably played by Elizabeth. The theme of homosexuality was handled softly. Another Tennessee

Taylor, as a southern belle, crowns Montgomery Clift, as a small town Indiana boy, in *Raintree County* (1957).

Williams movie followed, *Suddenly Last Summer*, 1959. Elizabeth looked flawlessly beautiful. *Butterfield 8*, 1960, won Elizabeth an Academy Award. At first she resisted playing the role of a call girl. But she realized there was a tragic side to her character and took the part. The Oscar may have been awarded to her partly from sympathy. She had fallen dramatically ill that year and nearly died. The illness turned public sympathy in her direction again and she was forgiven for marrying Eddie Fisher.

A new scandal was brewing, however. Elizabeth went to England to make *Cleopatra*, 1963. She was chosen for the role in what was expected to be one of the most lavish movies ever made because she was the screen's reigning brunette beauty and one of the most important celebrities Hollywood had ever produced. Rex Harrison was cast as Caesar and a classic Shakespearian actor named Richard Burton was scheduled to play Anthony. Elizabeth signed on to the project for a cool million.

What followed is legendary. Elizabeth and Richard fell in love. The movie which had cost umpteen millions in the first place grew ever more expensive as the antics of the stars slowed production. Richard Burton was an extraordinarily talented actor who had risen from the poverty of a Welsh mining town to become a major figure in English theater. A prodigious drinker, a man of great personal charm, he was as flamboyant as Mike Todd in his own way. There were 'incidents' with Eddie

Fisher. There were 'incidents' with Burton's wife, Sybil. The fans ate it up.

In 1964 Elizabeth married Burton. *Cleopatra* had opened to bad reviews and though it was not the smash its backers had hoped for, it eventually made money. Elizabeth improved enormously as an actress after her marriage to Burton, who introduced her to poetry and serious theater. Their life style continued to intrigue the public. They lived like potentates, traveling about with an entourage, making pots of money and spending lavishly. Mike Nichols directed them in Edward Albee's *Who's Afraid of Virginia Woolf?*, 1966. Elizabeth had the courage to look totally unglamorous in the role of a vicious yet pathetic wife. She played the part beautifully, winning a second Academy Award. The *Taming of the Shrew*, 1967, also starring Burton, revealed her as a desirable and earthy Katherine.

It was time for Elizabeth to make a new transition, however. She was now well into her 30s, an era as dangerous to a movie goddess as adolescence is to a child star. Some stars cling to beauty; Elizabeth did not. She allowed herself to mature into a grand character. It served her well with the public and even though she dropped out of the top ten box office attractions in the late 1960s, she continued to be a major force in the entertainment field.

Elizabeth made a good film, *Reflections in a Golden Eye*,

1967, with Marlon Brando. She did *The Comedians* with Burton, based on Graham Greene's novel of life in Haiti, 1967. *Boom!*, 1968, had the couple together before the cameras again but it fared poorly, making back barely one quarter of its cost. In *Secret Ceremony*, 1969, Elizabeth was cast as an aging whore attracted to Mia Farrow. *The Only Game in Town*, 1970, co-starring Warren Beatty, was filmed in Paris though set in Las Vegas. It was the last time she received a salary in the million dollar range.

Hammersmith is Out, 1972, made it apparent that the Burtons had lost their magic on film. So Elizabeth did a thriller on her own, *Night Watch*, 1973, co-starring Laurence Harvey, another old friend. The Burtons' intense but stormy relationship was beginning to fall apart. They were divorced in 1974. They remarried but it didn't work.

Elizabeth made *Ash Wednesday*, 1973, a film which would once have been called 'a woman's picture' about a love affair. Other movies followed, appealing chiefly to her most ardent fans, not the public in general. She made one excellent movie, *The Mirror Cracked*, 1980, which was based on an Agatha Christie mystery novel. Film legend Kim Novak was also in the movie. Elizabeth was doing television as well as making personal appearances by this time, since her movies were no longer a major draw. But her chief triumph was to come on Broadway.

The myth that Elizabeth couldn't act died hard, even though her many years in front of the camera had given her a magnificent grasp of film technique, as several of her later movies proved. Offered a chance to appear as Regina in Lillian Hellman's classic play, *The Little Foxes*, Elizabeth bravely took on the theatrical world. If the critics were out to get her, she changed their minds. Surrounding herself with a highly talented cast, she worked hard rehearsing the play, which concerns a greedy Southern family at the turn of the century.

The play was well-received, Elizabeth's performance applauded, and when the production reached Broadway, people queued up for tickets in droves. Though her personal relationship with Burton had changed, they could still work together. They did Noel Coward's *Private Lives* in New York. The show was a hit.

Whatever Elizabeth accomplished on screen or on stage, her personal life still glittered. She married Republican John Warner of Virginia, helping him campaign for the United States Senate. He won, and a new chapter opened in Elizabeth's life. They loved her in Washington.

Divorced again, she announced plans to marry a Mexican millionaire Victor Luna, a lawyer. As usual the announcement brought plenty of media attention. Who knows what surprises Elizabeth has in store for her fans next? With this lady, anything is possible.

She was once a little girl so lovely it broke your heart just to look at her. Then she became one of the most

The movie that started all the gossip about Elizabeth Taylor and Richard Burton—*Cleopatra* (1963).

Above: Three of the stars of *Giant* (1956)—Taylor, Rock Hudson and James Dean. This was Dean's last film.

Taylor as a prostitute in *Butterfield 8* (1960). She gave a magnificent performance, and won an Academy Award.

beautiful women in the world. Now in her 50s, she's become a kind of modern wife of Bath. Frankly fat, she loves to wear wildly unsuitable clothes, and she exudes a cheery vulgarity that makes her marvelous. She's had it all and she's done it all. She's Liz Taylor. Enough said.

Elizabeth Taylor: *There's One Born Every Minute* 42, *Lassie Come Home* 43, *Jane Eyre* 44, *The White Cliffs of Dover* 44, *National Velvet* 44, *Courage of Lassie* 46, *Cynthia* 47, *Life With Father* 47, *A Date With Judy* 48, *Julia Misbehaves* 48, *Little Women* 49, *Conspirator* 50, *The Big Hangover* 50, *Father of the Bride* 50, *Father's Little Dividend* 51, *Quo Vadis* 51, *Love is Better Than Ever* 52, *A Place in the Sun* 51, *The Light Fantastic* 51, *Ivanhoe* 52, *The Girl Who Had Everything* 53, *Rhapsody* 54, *Elephant Walk* 54, *Beau Brummel* 54, *The Last Time I Saw Paris* 54, *Giant* 56, *Raintree County* 57, *Cat on a Hot Tin Roof* 58, *Suddenly Last Summer* 59, *Butterfield 8* 60, *Scent of Mystery* 60, *Cleopatra* 63, *The VIPs* 63, *The Sandpiper* 65, *Who's Afraid of Virginia Woolf?* 66, *The Taming of the Shrew* 67, *Doctor Faustus* 67, *The Comedians* 67, *Reflections in a Golden Eye* 67, *Boom* 68, *Secret Ceremony* 69, *The Only Game in Town* 70, *Under Milkwood* 71, *Zee and Company* 72, *Hammersmith Is Out* 72, *Night Watch* 73, *Ash Wednesday* 73, *Driver's Seat* 74, *The Blue Bird* 76, *Divorce His; Divorce Hers* 73, *Victory at Entebbe* 76, *A Little Night Music* 76, *Winter Kills* 79, *Return Engagement* 78, *The Mirror Cracked* 80, *Between Friends* 80.

Above: She won another Oscar for *Who's Afraid of Virginia Woolf?* (1966).   *Below:* She starred with Burton again in *The Comedians* (1967).

Lana Turner, who was christened 'America's Sweater Girl.'